InvestiDate: How to Investigate Your Date

MARIA CODER

Printed in the United States of America

ISBN-13: 978-1468162424
ISBN-10: 146816242X

Edited by Andrew Craft

Book layout and design by Rachel Liu

Dedication

....

To my mom, dad, and brother, the best
safety net of all;

and my closest friends, trusted urban confidantes,
who rally at a moment's notice;

and to all the single men and women who've
ever had a hunch, a bad experience, or a colossal
disappointment, I hope you'll dust yourselves off,
arm yourselves with information, and keep on going.

InvestiDate:
How to Investigate
Your Date

table of contents

Introduction, aka why I wrote this book

"SOMEONE MUST'VE done something really bad to you," that's the first thing I usually hear when I tell people I started InvestiDate. And yes, they're right, someone did. But he's not the reason I started this book, he's the reason I finished it.

I'm no wimp. I've outrun a hurricane, canceled a wedding, and picked myself up a time or two but nothing could've prepared me for that fateful August day.

My boyfriend called in a panic, he wanted to know if I was on my way to his apartment. I wasn't. I was half way to my apartment but something about the conversation was weird. He said he only asked because if I were on my way to his place, he didn't want me waiting for "hours and hours and hours" while he went to fix a computer for a client. He reminded me that his house was my house and I was welcome there whenever I wanted, and of course, that's why he'd given me a key.

"I'll call you tomorrow to make an appointment," he said.

"An appointment?" I asked.

"Yeah," he said.

"Since when do we make appointments to see each other?" I asked.

I should've known.

He promised he'd call me once he finished his job but my instinct kicked in when I realized he'd left to go to his job and hadn't called; he always called en route. It was 7 pm.

At 2 am a little voice from deep inside kept saying "Get your rear to Brooklyn." And that's what I did.

At 4:30 am I woke his mom, apologetically. I called and said I hadn't heard from her son and asked if she'd heard anything. I'd explained the car had broken down while we were in it the night before and this all seemed so out-of-character.

At 6 am I was resting on his bed, thinking, when I noticed an opened box of condoms by the TV. *How odd,* I thought.

Come 7 am his mom and I were calling his cell phone non-stop. English her second language, she asked that I call hospital emergency rooms. I moved to his computer for the first time all night to get on the Internet and locate phone numbers to start a massive *find the boyfriend* campaign.

It must've been around 8 am when it occurred to me that maybe he'd posted something on Facebook. I went to Facebook.com to log into my account but up popped his account with his last chat window wide open.

I would've fallen if I weren't sitting—I am sure of it.

There, in black and white and riddled with typos, my boyfriend was getting directions to another woman's home. He who was always strapped for cash was willing to drive more than an hour each way. The conversation started at the time he'd called in a panic seeking my whereabouts earlier in the day; my cell phone would corroborate. In the chat window, he gave her his cell phone, not once but twice, in case she missed it before. He ended the message in Spanish with: anticipate my kisses.

Out of the corner of my eye I saw his Facebook inbox, a growing point of contention in our relationship. I didn't understand why he minimized the screen every time I was near. But now clarity was a click away. Adrenaline high, I clicked and found nearly three dozen emails—solicitations, meeting requests, you name it. It was disturbing. It was disgusting. It was plain devastating.

"Do you know where he is?" his mom asked.

"Yes," I said, thinking what to say. Then a thought: why cover for him? "He's having sex with this woman," I pointed at the thumbnail photo.

"No, I don't know that woman," she said, hovering behind me.

"Apparently, neither does he," I said.

I don't know how I managed to get up and get out

but I did. I wasn't alone. My grandma was there. It sounds Twilight-zone-ish; I know. I swear to you she was there, in spirit, watching over me. She helped me toss my things into a small suitcase, which ironically, was my mom's suitcase that I'd recently lent him for a trip. It was the only empty bag in sight.

I was crying uncontrollably. I still hadn't realized the intricacy of the web of lies he'd woven. It would take an impromptu trip of his to Mexico for me to piece it all together—the early morning parking tickets near his married friend's home, the gaping holes in his stories, his occasional forgetfulness, his temper flare ups, his inexplicable disappearing acts, the sleazy Twitter followers, the whole nine yards. I felt so stupid. I had seen it but I thought my book, this book, started six years earlier, was playing tricks with my head, so I intentionally set aside what I knew. Stupid girl.

His mom kept asking me to stay. She was talking a mile a minute, desperately making a very flimsy case for her son. *Pick a team, lady* was all I was thinking; I couldn't process a single word she said.

And then, just as I was leaving I saw my brand new professional grade blow dryer sitting on the vanity—what to do? Make a clean break or grab it? Laughter filled my head as I turned around, opened my mom's suitcase, and reached for my blower. *Let's be reasonable now*, I thought.

And that moment is when I knew I would be alright but it would be a long time before I got there.

There are other details, a slew, a bunch, a heap, a pack—too many to list. Suffice it to say, he gave me a good kick in the pants. He reminded me why I started

InvestiDate. It was so people like you and me wouldn't waste any more precious time over the losers, the worthless, the immature. It was to protect the good-hearted from the liars, the criminals, the cheats. It was to prevent those terrible, awful, no-good things you hear about in the news from happening to us.

After all, there are a lot of *us*. There are 96 million people in the United States who are unattached, which means for every 100 single women, there are 88 unmarried men, according to census data. Forty million singles date online. I may indeed be single but I am not alone; we're in this together.

So, I'm sure you'll join me in total amazement when I tell you what happened next.

He called me a week later. I didn't want to pick up but I missed his voice and I thought maybe, just maybe, I was finally getting an apology. Closure served a la mea culpa, a form of 'hey I'm a pendejo and I'm so sorry,' some shred of human semblance.

But no; he called to tell me this was all my fault.

"Are you kidding me?" I asked.

"No," he said. *"This is all your fault."*

"How? How is this possibly my fault?"

"You found the messages," he said.

"You wrote the messages! You created them!" I said, exasperatedly.

"Oh, and another thing, your InvestiDate idea is stupid.

Don't even try it. You'll fail miserably."

I hung up, powered on my laptop, and got back to work.

Read my lips

THE WORDS WE say are a teeny tiny fraction of what we communicate to others. Bite your lip; for instance, and you signal romantic interest. Purse your lips; however, and you appear deep in thought. While the words we choose are telling, how we deliver those words, says even more. Think about it: how many times have you heard someone say, "It's not what you said, it's *how* you said it?"

Turns out, it's easy to fib and speak untruths but it's not so easy for your body to go along for the ride. It's the same for your date's.

Let's listen as 26-year-old Kristie tells her friend about Jim, a 28-year-old attractive, businessman whom she met at a co-worker's going away party.

Jim was the life of the party. He had everyone laughing hysterically. It was one punch line after another, it was as if he had an endless stream of jokes and magic tricks up his sleeve. At one point, I swear I saw the pink Energizer Rabbit streaming across my head. I was hooked. Before I knew it we'd exchanged phone numbers.

On our first date, he took me to an expensive Italian restaurant. He told me how much he loved vintage wines and how next summer he was planning a trip to Napa. I could feel myself leaning forward in my seat. You know, I've always wanted to go to wine country. It was an excellent date, full of interesting conversation. He asked me about my favorite movies and books. He wanted to know all about my yoga class even though it wasn't really his thing. He talked so fast I was on the edge of my seat trying to keep up—literally. I could feel the wood branding its mark in my thigh. At one point my chair slightly tipped forward! It was kind of embarrassing so I was relieved the two times Jim excused himself to use the restroom. I actually thought he was fighting a cold since he kept sniffing but was impressed he seemed so upbeat if he were feeling under the weather. All in all, the perfect first date—a ten on a scale of one to ten. He walked me to my car, gave me a quick peck on the lips and said he'd call me about doing something next Saturday.

It's only been two days and I haven't heard but I'm obsessively checking my cell phone. I am sure he will call soon.

And call he did. On their second date, Jim invited Kristie to a salsa club. Both beginners, they arrived early for the free class. Kristie wore her little black dress, fire engine red heels, and just the right amount of cherry-flavored lip gloss.

He looked soooooo good. He was wearing this black, button down, shirt with interesting pockets and faded blue jeans. He was so uninhibited, he'd try all the steps, everything. I felt like a fish out of water but not Jim. He would've done the funky chicken if you'd asked him! At one point he excused himself to use the restroom and came back with a rum and coke. He offered me a sip but it was too strong for me. I noticed he turned around and popped a pill. It was like a white round pill. I asked if he was sick and he said no. "Allergies," I asked? He shook his head no, then pointed up to the ceiling to kind of signal the song that was starting was one that he liked. He took a big gulp of his drink, set it down and grabbed my arm. We must've danced seven songs in a row. Maybe eight! My peep-toe heels begged for mercy. I asked to take a breather.

As I sat there breathless Jim seemed unfazed, dancing beside me, using my arm as an axle to spin around. You could tell he was just getting started. How was that possible? I started to wonder about the pill. What was it? Was it safe to drink such a strong rum and coke with it? I guess I got distracted watching the better dancers because Jim had moved on to his third drink—a shot of something or other. I told him I was wiped out. He offered to drive me home but he seemed bordering tipsy. I told him I thought we should share a cab. I meant we should share a cab to each of our own respective homes but he took it as an invitation. And well, I mentioned he looked really good right? What can I say, he stayed over.

The next morning I playfully nudged him awake. I had to go to meet my mom for brunch and it was too late to call it off. I was shocked when he got pissy! He woke up in such a bad mood. Twice he said that he'd left his jeans on that big oversized chair in my bedroom and that I'd moved them to the living room.

At first I thought he was joking and the punch line was going over my head but no, he meant it! But why would I move his stuff then lie about it? It was ridiculous. I guess it was when he realized just how ridiculous it sounded that he said "got you," laughed it off and started to back pedal. He kissed me on the forehead and said he had a great time and would call me later. Then as he was leaving he stubbed his toe on that raised part of the doorway between my bedroom and the living room. His gut reaction was to punch the wall. He left a dent and everything. He's called four times already and I've let it go to voicemail. I just don't know what to make of it. It seems controlling. Or maybe just excessive? Whatever it is, I don't like it.

Hesitant to be judgmental, Kristie returned Jim's last call. He told her about a comedy show on Friday he'd been dying to see and would love to take her. Giving him the benefit of the doubt, Kristie agreed to meet Jim once more. When she got to the club, Jim was already inside nursing a beer. He seemed a little hyper but since he always seemed energized, Kristie figured it was normal. Again, she told her friend all about it.

'Hang on a second,' he said, when the hostess said our table was ready. I could've sworn I saw him pop something in his mouth again. I couldn't tell if it was like a mint or if it was that same white pill from last time.

'Are you feeling alright?' I asked. 'Was that Claritin?"'

'Fine,' he said, and kissed my cheek. 'Shall we?' he pointed toward the path behind the hostess.

So I followed. It was a good show and I love comedy

but I couldn't really get into it. I just wanted to go home. At the end of the show, I said I had an early yoga class the next day and needed to get going. I don't think he completely bought it. I don't know why I said it, really. I don't have yoga on Saturdays. I'm kicking myself now. He's cute and available and straight and those are so hard to come by! I keep checking my phone but he hasn't called.

Kristie was on to something. Even if she couldn't articulate or even identify her thoughts as doubt or skepticism, she was right on. She suspected something about pill use and alcohol intake yet she was afraid to judge a book by its cover. And probably afraid that what she might discover could leave her, well, dateless.

And yet, despite the modern day approach to giving someone a chance, sometimes a girl really needs to know what she's dealing with. Accepting that no one is perfect, you should still know what level of imperfection you can deal with. Or shall we say, what dose?

In this day and age of stock market crashes, high unemployment, low workload, and dizzying deadlines it makes sense that some (OK, a lot) of men (and women) may need to be on legitimately prescribed, doctor-supervised, medication. But if you're dating a pill-popping guy and you haven't had a chance to accidentally lose your lipstick inside his bathroom cabinet, you may want to take a good look at one of those pesky little pills while he fetches a glass of water (or another Cuba Libre).

Most medicines are marked, or imprinted, so that they can be identified. These imprints can include a brand's logo, numerical digit or alphabet character. WebMd.com has a free Pill Identifier page where you simply fill in what you know of the drug and you're on your way to getting some answers. Another site created to help us decode the jargon is www.drugid.info. Pharmacists there charge a small fee, starting at $9.95 to identify up to five drugs within one year.

Once you've got the name of the pill, you can easily search on Google, or any search engine, to read more about it. If you suspect the pills aren't exactly for proper medical use, visit StreetDrugs.org. Here you'll see photos of various kinds of drugs, learn their multiple names, alternative uses, and how they're bought and sold.

In Jim's case, chances are he was hooked on speed. The white, round, pill is a dextroamphetamine and acts as a psychostimulant drug, which is known to produce increased wakefulness and suppress fatigue. Mixing this type of drug with alcohol is dangerous and can be deadly. Speed makes people feel wide awake and chatty. It makes sense that Kristie couldn't keep up with Jim's quick talk and endless energy.

Amphetamines also have diuretic properties and similar to alcohol, can cause an increase in urination. It's nearly impossible to get a good night's sleep on speed too. The come-down can make users feel irritable and depressed for a day or two. Another giveaway was the sniffing—someone who takes speed sniffs a lot in a short amount of time.

If you're dating someone with unusual symptoms and are stumped as to what's going on, you could just flat out ask why he pops those pills. If the answer leaves you uneasy, a strand of freshly plucked hair could prove useful with a $59.95 Psychemedics drug test (this test is usually marketed toward teens but do men really ever grow up?); www.drugfreeteenagers.com.

Investigators say that an open-ended question is much better than a direct one.

"When you question someone, don't ever give them a clue," says Tony Pacheco Ortiz, a retired supervisor and special agent for Immigrations and Customs Enforcement, the Human Trafficking Division of Homeland Security. "Don't ask is that Claritin?" Instead say "I've been sniffing a lot too lately. What's that you got there? It might help me."

Pacheco Ortiz warns daters to keep a look out for eyes that frequently seem glazed over, dilated pupils, arms with needle pricks, and wandering eye contact during specific questions. An extra long pinkie nail could mean a cocaine or tobacco habit to either scoop the powder or split blunt paper. He admits it's nearly impossible to gauge a recreational drug user or even an addict, unless you're in a real relationship and spend enough time to notice little things. "But a bunch of circumstantial evidence will lead you to a fact," he says.

"Keep an eye on marijuana users," stresses Pacheco Ortiz. "It usually starts with marijuana. It's the most innocent of the drugs but it's a starter drug, a gateway drug, it doesn't lead to anything good."

The most dangerous drugs, he says, are heroin, cocaine, oxycontin and crystal meth. Though all medicine when abused is lethal.

Keeping a journal with a few key words or phrases can be a tremendous help. If Kristie had jotted down sniffing, white pill, high energy, multiple drinks, gorgeous smile— and seen similar key words on all three dates, she may have detected a pattern. Frequently women say "He looked so good on paper," meaning great job, great degree, great apartment. Perhaps a closer look reveals he's not so hot on paper after all!

And honestly, if you've spun your wheels this far in a quest for answers, you may want to move on. Each time Kristie asked about the drug she was thrown off course by the answer. Not once did Jim attempt to answer her question or provide a morsel of comfort. Isn't that itself a red flag?

Perhaps there's reassurance in knowing that time reveals truth. Liars need to have incredible memories to keep their stories straight. To be fair, Jim had not lied once to Kristie. He omitted information but he never flat out fibbed. He was asked if he had allergies and he said no. He was asked if he took Claritin and he again said no. Jim did not volunteer incriminating information and he did avoid answering specific questions. Unfortunately, there's no way for Kristie to know for sure if Jim is an occasional drug user, a habitual drug user, or worse, an addict? Just how long should she wait to gather clues? One more week? A month? Six months? Two years? She's not getting any younger, you know.

Unsure what to do, Kristie arranged a dinner date with Jim. On the drive to the restaurant she tried to visualize a scale and put Jim's good points on one side and his flaws on the other. She didn't get very far. Each time she found one positive thing, she'd add a negative and for each negative, she'd find a positive. Jim was neck-and-neck with himself. She thought about the white pills and thought perhaps they were purely recreational. Maybe Jim was just going through some sort of rough patch; *everyone goes through rough patches,* she told herself. In college, she'd tried marijuana, and she grew out of it—hadn't touched the stuff since. Kristie imagined how stressful it must be to work in such a cutthroat business world. *Maybe Jim just needs a vacation.*

As Kristie struggled to find a parking spot, she glanced at her watch, relieved to have arrived 10-minutes early so as to gather her thoughts and take a deep breath. *Don't turn this into a thing,* she mumbled under her breath. *It's not that big a deal.*

Inside the restaurant, the host took her to a small table near the back. Kristie glanced through the menu trying to choose an appetizer she and Jim could share, since she had nothing better to do and was trying not to think about that thing she wasn't supposed to be thinking about. The waitress popped by to take her drink order but Kristie said she'd stick with water until her date arrived. Fifteen-minutes later, the waitress stopped by again.

"Are you sure I can't get you anything while you wait?" asks the waitress.

"No thanks, I'm fine," says Kristie.

She glanced at her watch and realized Jim was now another 25-minutes late. Worried, she double-checked her phone. She hadn't heard it ring but maybe the reception wasn't as strong from where she was sitting. How bizarre. Jim's punctuality was one of his good points. Kristie picked up the phone and called Jim but it rang and rang until his voicemail kicked in. She left a message. She figured she'd wait 10-more minutes- maybe he was stuck in traffic or something. After all, he'd confirmed the dinner the night before.

Now 10 more minutes later, Jim was still nowhere to be found. Kristie called again and again got voicemail.

Where the hell was Jim? She browsed the local headlines on the Internet, maybe there had been an accident. Ten-minutes later and no answer on her third call, all Kristie could think was—*there better have been an accident!*

Deflated and famished, Kristie went home. She was talking with a friend on the phone, recounting how she got stood up, when she got another call: Jim. Kristie clicked over.

"I saw you called Kris, what's up?" shouts Jim.

"What's up?" asks Kristie, now angry. "Where are you?"

"I'm with the guys at a bar, watching the game," says Jim, completely unfazed.

"What about our dinner? I waited for you. I was worried sick."

"What are you talking about?" asks Jim. His voice sounding slightly slurred. "What dinner? That's not tonight."

"Ugh, good night, Jim," says Kristie, then she hangs up.

In that moment, Kristie realized life's too short to put up with this drama. She thought about the past few dates with Jim and the roller coaster she'd been on. Instead of wondering: *Does he like me? Does he not like me?* She'd spent more time wondering: *Is he hooked on drugs? Is he not hooked on drugs?* She'd been accused of moving a pair of jeans into another room and she'd been stood up, all in less than three weeks. Her pseudo-boyfriend had already forgotten their dinner plans, choosing to watch the game with his friends. Kristie wondered if Jim even remembered their date this morning or if a little white pill had anything to do with his memory lapse. Then she realized she was doing it again—wondering. *How much time do I have left to waste wondering?* she wondered. It was then and there that Kristie decided to move on. Jim was a great guy, smart, sexy, straight, attractive but this stuff, the bad stuff, this is the type of stuff that doesn't get better.

> *"If I have to roll the dice on this one," she told her friend. "I'll cut my losses." Then Kristie put the cordless phone on the charger and walked into the kitchen where she made herself a very big sandwich.*

Kristie's not the only person taking control of how she spends her time. Claudia is another savvy gal unwilling to spend her days or nights trying to change somebody.

A 31-year-old woman living in Westchester, New York, Claudia is a die-hard Democrat. She marches for gay rights and signs petitions for changes she wishes to help enact. She often tells her friends she doesn't want a Republican in the White House and she certainly doesn't want him in her bed. Her stance is clear and her desire to find someone of her same political belief system is strong.

This isn't up for debate. A Republican or an Independent simply won't do. In fact, she dumped her last boyfriend, last election, for failing to vote. She means business and yet, a true diplomat, she's aware of how politically incorrect it is to ask someone about their political beliefs; having met Michael on an online dating site, it's hard to tell his leanings. On her first date, the intelligent, 33-year-old Texan transplant hints that he's full throttle behind Leftist efforts. Michael is passionate and naturally seductive; he's a fan of country music (as is Claudia). She thinks she may have just found a Democratic cowboy. What could be better?

Let's pop in on Cowboy Michael now.

"I think it's impressive that you hand-made signs and went on pilgrimage to Washington," says Michael. It's so important that you keep your right to choose. Isn't it ironic how men feel they can dictate whether or not a woman may abort an embryo? It seems so 17th Century. I wasn't able to attend the march but I thought about it. I wrote a check to the National Association of Women (NOW). Does that count?"

Claudia can't believe her ears. What are the odds? She feels a broad smile come across her face. Michael doesn't miss a beat.

"You have a really beautiful smile," he says.

Euphoric after her date, Claudia conference calls her two best friends. Impressed that Michael has a Southern twang and a Democratic vote, they couldn't be happier for their dear friend. They want to know everything, down to the last detail—What he does for a living? How old is he? How long has he been in New York? What part of Westchester County does he live in? What part of Texas did he come from? The list goes on. Then one of her friends, Emma, asks for his last name. She jots down the answer.

It doesn't take long before Emma finds a hole in the heart of Texas. Emma, pretty much a born snoop, is always looking out for the best interests of her close friends. After getting off the phone she searches for information on Michael. NOW is a charity but it doesn't readily list members and donors. Determined, Emma stumbles on the Web site www.OpenSecrets.org, which tracks political donations and finds a donor lookup section. She types in Michael's name and selects New York as a state. Nothing comes up. OK, she figures maybe his contribution to NOW is his only contribution to Leftist movements. That's acceptable. *For someone from the predominantly Republican state of Texas, it's even surprising,* she thinks out loud. Then a little light bulb flashes above her head—TEXAS. She searches again, types in Michael's full name and this time selects the state of Texas. She finds that Michael has donated upward of $500 toward a Republican candidate. Her stomach drops—what to tell Claudia? Emma takes a look at the contributor column to double-check the city in Texas. Sure enough, it's Austin, just like Claudia had said he'd said. The occupation column confirms her suspicion: Michael is either a born again Democrat or a big fat liar. Emma calls Claudia to tell her the news and shares the Web site. Claudia is bummed but decides to give Michael a good ol' second try

A few days later, Michael texts Claudia to ask if she'd like to meet for happy hour after work. Claudia agrees—but this time, she has a clear agenda. She wants to find out from the horse's mouth if he's a Democratic donkey or a Republican elephant.

Sitting at the bar, Claudia mentions how she's contributed in previous years to presidential campaigns. This isn't entirely true. Claudia has never contributed financially but feels her hands-on involvement and volunteer work is worth more than money and carefully chooses her words. Let's listen in.

"Me too," says Michael. It seems somewhere between his second round of drinks and his talk of a road trip with some buddies out West, he forgot about party

lines and ended up with enough rope to lasso himself into one big blur.

"We actually ran into a man outside a restaurant in Phoenix talking about John McCain and Sarah (Palin) and I approached him to ask if he was a political enthusiast or a relation. He seemed to know so much. He told my buddies and me that John was a close friend. Now, who knows if that were true but I told him we were rooting for his buddy and that beauty queen maverick of his."

Claudia didn't want to be rude and cut him off but after that date, she had no issue cutting him loose. The next time Cowboy Michael called, Claudia told him she was busy. She said that twice more before Michael went away.

Claudia's approach was quite customary. It seems a few drinks and some easy chatter lowers one's guard and makes a person more susceptible to uncensored talk. Plus, since this was a second date, Michael was probably less nervous to begin with. There are; however, other ways that Claudia could have arrived at the same conclusion.

Had she poked and prodded at Michael's stance on certain issues, then (presuming he were honest) she could have used the answers to complete a questionnaire that rates party affiliation, like the one at PoliticalCompass.org or the "What Political Party is Right for You?" quiz at www.quizrocket.com/political-party-quiz.

Lastly, Claudia could have simply discussed in detail something gross. Yes, gross as in disgusting. Apparently, according to a study by Yoel Inbar and David A. Pizarro of Cornell University and Paul Bloom of Yale, people who squirm at the sight of bugs, blood, and guts are more likely to be politically conservative.

Psychology professor David Pizarro and his colleagues surveyed 181 U.S. adults from politically mixed swing states. They used a Disgust Sensitivity Scale (DSS), to judge, well, disgust, sensitivity, and political ideology (also on a scale). Researchers found a correlation between being more easily disgusted and political conservatism. Then they surveyed 91 Cornell undergraduates with the DSS, and asked questions about their stance on gay marriage, abortion, gun control, labor unions, tax cuts and affirmative action. Those who were most disgusted were more likely to oppose gay marriage and abortion.

Questions used in the study included dilemmas such as: whether and in what circumstances you might be willing to try eating monkey meat or how disgusted you'd feel if a friend offered you a piece of chocolate shaped like dog-doo. If you'd like to check the test against your own political preferences, Professor Pizarro has uploaded the study to his Web site at www.Peezer.net. A second study among 25,000 Americans as well as people from more than a hundred countries, which corroborates those findings will be posted there soon.

There are other situations in which you have to bite your tongue because getting an answer through a straightforward Q&A could be incredibly insulting. Such is the case for Ed.

Ed is 52-years-old and a savvy businessman. He owns multiple properties along Miami's waterfront. Divorced with two college-aged children, he is busy but lonely. He hopes to meet someone genuine and exciting.

While reading a local upscale magazine, Ed stumbles on some personal ads near the back. After reading a few, he decides to call the magazine and place his own ad. The magazine assigns Ed a voicemail number and he waits eagerly for the issue with his ad to come out to see what kinds of responses he gets.

When the magazine hits the newsstands, Ed calls his voicemail to check if he has any messages. He's happily surprised to find out he has four calls. One that stands out is from a 33-year-old woman named Amber. The message is short and sweet and Amber sounds stunning. After fumbling a bit, Ed decides to call Amber and ask to meet her at a lounge next Friday.

Happy as a clam, Ed calls his pal Steve to tell him the great news. Steve, perhaps a bit jealous, instantly presumes Amber is either a gold digger or a hooker.

"Why would she want to date a 52-year-old guy like you?" asks Steve. "And you found her through a magazine ad? Come on!"

"I hadn't thought of all that," says Ed. "I don't know."

Once full of hope and good cheer, Ed is now uneasy. *Could his pal be right? Is Amber after his money? Did his ad scream money?* Unsure, he reaches for the magazine and re-reads his words. Nope. He decides to ignore his friend. After all, it's just a date and he's not looking to tie the knot anytime soon.

Friday rolls around and Ed arrives at the lounge early. He sits in a nook from where he can watch people arrive and orders a gin and tonic to calm his first date jitters. It's been a long time since Ed's been on a date. He stares at the door like an owl—eyes wide, fixed on every person that enters the room. When Amber arrives he spots her instantly and walks toward her. She kisses him on the cheek and follows him back to his seating nook.

Ed can't believe his eyes. Amber is absolutely gorgeous. Blonde-ish hair, low cut black blouse, jeans, a beautiful red and pink necklace and a small clutch. In no time they're talking and laughing and ordering appetizers. Ed asks Amber what she'd like to drink and she asks for a diet coke. Ed orders another gin and tonic. Two hours later, the pair seems to have really hit it off. Three hours later, Amber checks her watch and says she needs to get going. Ed kisses her on the cheek and invites her to dinner and a movie next Tuesday. Amber happily makes note of her date in her Blackberry and they part ways.

When Ed returns home, he sees a message from Steve on his home phone and returns the call. Let's listen in.

"She was positively delightful. Beautiful. Long blonde hair, a fabulous figure. She showed some skin in a nice low cut blouse. She was funny and intelligent; she definitely didn't seem 33. Did you know there's a monastery in Aventura? She was telling me all about how her brother married his college sweetheart at a little chapel there and apparently, the property was built abroad, disassembled, numbered, then shipped to the U.S. and reassembled piece-by-piece, like a jigsaw puzzle. I'm a property guy. How did I not know this? Anyway, I'm seeing her again on Tuesday—dinner and movie."

Steve is unconvinced. "Did her boobs scream plastic surgery?" he asks, half joking, half green with envy.

"No Stevie. Settle down," says Ed.

"I'm just saying how do you know? What if she's one of those women who go around marrying rich men and killing them for their money? Or what if she marries you and walks away with all your remaining property? What if your son says 'Hey dad, my new mom is 14-years older than me.' I mean, have you even thought this through? The implications? If she's a hooker, what are the legalities? Or shall I say illegalities?"

Ed decides he's heard enough. "Talk later, Steve, chill out."

Tuesday rolls around and over dinner, Amber asks more questions about Ed's job and hobbies. The second he mentions art, Amber tells him how she minored in art history. She asks if his family has collected art or if this is a new hobby. Suddenly, Ed feels uncomfortable. He thinks of Steve and wonders if Amber is after a pay day. *Is she a hooker looking for a client or a gold digger that would like nothing more than to take him to the cleaners?* Listen to how it unfolds...

"Why do you ask?" asks Ed.

"Oh," retorts Amber, caught off guard. "I don't know. I was just making conversation, I guess."

"It's a new thing," snaps Ed.

"Well, good for you," says Amber. "I'm a huge fan of Romero Britto. I've always wanted an original but they are so expensive. I have a few framed posters at home instead but I love them as if they were the real thing."

Ed sits back in his seat. Amber takes notice.

"Ed, are you OK?"

"Look, I don't know what your plan is but I'm just looking to date somebody."

Amber sits up "Pardon me? I don't like your tone. What exactly do you mean, Ed?"

"My friend Steve warned me about this. I guess he's right," says Ed.

"Right about what, Ed?" Amber looks fuming mad.

"You're lovely but I am not looking for a trophy girlfriend. I'm after a real connection."

Horrified, Amber drops the fork she was holding in her hand. "You think I'm after your money?" she asks, in complete dismay.

"Aren't you?" asks Ed.

"No. No I'm not," says Amber, standing up to leave.

Ed quickly stands too. "Wait," he says, his hand on her wrist. "Let me explain."

"You have two seconds so make it good," she says, her eyes now narrow.

"My buddy Steve thinks the only reason an attractive 33-year-old woman like you would be interested in an old geyser like me is because I'm financially well-off. I had a great time with you and told him I thought you were fantastic. I guess the way you phrased your art question made me think you were prying into my finances. He filled my head with garbage about

escorts and gold diggers. I don't really think that of you but your question threw me off and I apologize. It was wrong of me."

"Ahh man," says Amber. "I am not an escort! I'm also not after your money! I am sick of dating men my age who act like boys. I'm looking for a grown man. Sure, I'd like for him to be financially secure but I am not looking for a business opportunity. I asked about the art just to ask. I'm not used to talking with men who collect art and I was just trying to find something intelligent to say. Plus I studied art and I am genuinely interested in it. I guess it's just as difficult for a 30-something to date as it is for a 50-something to date," she shrugs.

"I'm sorry," says Ed. "I mean it. I am really, really sorry. How can I make it up to you?"

"Well, you could buy me a Britto," says Amber, letting out a loud laugh.

Having addressed the issue, Ed and Amber empathized with each other and their date went from awkward to amazing. In fact, on their next date Ed took Amber to Britto Central, an art gallery in Miami Beach that showcases the artist's work.

Ed's imagination got the better of him. It also almost ruined a perfectly good thing.

"It's not always simply about maturity or responsibility," explains Patrick Wanis, PhD, human behavior and relationship expert. Sometimes a woman seeks a different type of safety blanket. "Sometimes it's also because the woman feels there's less chance of him dumping her for a younger woman, because she is the younger woman. She is the treasure."

Wanis suggests if you're unsure of someone's intentions, you ask questions and listen carefully as they speak. Check their eye contact—it's natural for someone to blink and look away. "If they never break eye contact with you, it is likely they are trying to deceive or manipulate you," says Wanis. When you ask your date about a childhood memory, he or she is likely to look up to their left as they access their photo memory. If they're trying to remember what something or someone sounded like, their eyes will cross horizontally to their left. If they're mumbling, the eyes tend to look down.

Make sure you feel the person too—and that doesn't mean you physically touch them, it means you use your sixth sense. Are you uneasy in their presence? Are you leaning in wanting to know more or physically pushing back to separate from the situation? Gauge your own body language as much as you gauge their body speak. Are your arms crossed in an unspoken self-defense mechanism? Are you annoyed, defensive, or just cold? "Listen to your initial intuition—it is never wrong," says Wanis. "And beware of trying to shut down or ignore your intuition with logic, reasoning, or justification."

Generally speaking, hookers and gold diggers don't need to be won over. To them, everything you say is funny and charming. If you're not proverbially hunting and the woman has fallen prey, watch out.

If her purse is so small barely anything fits in there, she could also be a working girl, and charge by the hour. If she says anything that insinuates 500 reasons why you should date her, she's telling you it's $500 an hour to continue the date.

In Ed's case, Amber was truly interested in him, not his cash. But it really was tough to tell. While Amber didn't seem like a hooker; a gold digger wasn't as clear a call. She did phrase her art question rather unusually. Still, she stayed to hash it out. When Ed accused her of being after his money, she became visibly upset and dropped her fork, an involuntary jaunt to reality. It seemed there was no turning back for a moment there.

"If you really want to know if a woman is into you, watch how her body progressively changes," says Wanis. "If she progressively and gradually starts turning her body into you, she probably genuinely likes you. If she turns away, you've turned her off." When she crosses her legs, where does her knee face? Does it face you or away? If she touches her wrist or her neck it's an act of vulnerability. Wanis says in that case, "she's not just flirting with you but it's almost like an act of submission." If she rests her chin on both her hands she's completely intrigued. This doesn't mean she's romantically smitten but whatever you've said has her fully engaged.

Also pay close attention to her handbag. While a tiny bag may signal a pro, a purse is an easy way for a woman to show off herself and her style.

In general, an expendable bag with zippers and pockets is for young, 9-to-5ers that want to be cute yet practical. A designer brand, like Coach or Louis Vuitton, displays a certain level of financial reach. Ladies who tote this type of arm candy are either well-off or like the finer things. A cross-body purse with removable straps that pulls double-duty as a clutch is for a woman-on-the go who needs to quickly transition from office apropos to a night on the town. An oversized bag usually points to a disorganized person who totes around various possessions—many of which are unnecessary at the time. Remember to factor in location. A large bag in cities like Boston, Chicago, Washington D.C., and New York is much more customary as days and distances are long and women aren't exactly able to leave things in their non-existent cars or pop home before a date for items they may need to glam it up.

Also remember, not all prostitutes are women. There are male prostitutes and escorts too.

Wanis, often interviewed on television about celebrity body language, has several helpful articles on his Web site (www.PatrickWanis.com) that may help you properly "diagnose" your date. He also offers a paid service where you may submit photos of yourself with your date and he'll analyze the body language, like he would for a story on pop princess Britney Spears for a mainstream magazine.

Whatever you do, be careful what you insinuate. Ed was lucky Amber was so understanding. Just about any other man would have had a drink poured over his head. No one likes to be falsely accused.

Sometimes a little purse is just a little purse.

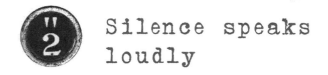

Silence speaks loudly

FROM TIME TO time, there is an elephant in the room. Have you ever felt tense in a situation knowing full well you weren't the only one to sense it? Sometimes the most telling information is what's unsaid. Listen carefully to the gaps in the story—what's been skirted, purposely avoided, or masked using clever innuendo. Then figure out why—silently, of course.

Take Sharon; for instance. The 33 year-old accountant met Angelo, a very well-dressed, extremely sexy Italian professor at a friend's birthday party.

"He's off the boat," a friend whispers into Sharon's ear. "Literally, he just got to New York City two-weeks ago, Steve says he's the most popular professor on campus," she says as she winks then walks away. Within minutes, Sharon's friend has grabbed Angelo by the arm and personally introduced him to her.

A few days later Sharon called her friend to fill her in on her first date.

"I still can't believe my luck. Angelo is incredible; so charming and animated. He chose the Metropolitan Museum of Art for our first date! He chose it! I can't believe it. He actually knew about the painters, the sculptors, and the history of the museum. You'd think he studied art history, not science. I absolutely loved his accent—I mean, half the time I didn't quite understand what he was saying but ha! That's the best part! I feel kinda bad for his pre-med students though. Anyway, we're going out again next week. Some foreign film, then dinner."

Sharon is elated. What luck—she's found this great guy, her first date went better than expected and she already has plans for a second date. Things are progressing nicely. Then on date number two she notices how chatty Angelo is with the male waiter and bus boy. At first, she thinks he's being his usual, friendly, Italian-self. Then she notices the waiter rubs his hand on Angelo's shoulder-twice. While the gesture catches Sharon off-guard, Angelo doesn't flinch. Could her sexy Italian be gay? Perplexed, she calls her friend to tiptoe around the issue.

"So last night at dinner the waiter put his hand on Angelo's shoulder twice," says Sharon.

"Who cares? It's not like he initiated it. Go somewhere else next time," says her friend.

"No, no, not the waitress," explains Sharon. "The WAITER."

"Oh, well, so what?"

"I think that Angelo liked it. He didn't flinch. He seemed totally comfortable," says Sharon.

"Well, you know Italians. They talk with their hands. He probably didn't think anything of it. Do you?"

"Um, yeah. I mean, OK, it could be an Italian thing but the boy can dress. He wears skinny jeans, he knows the Met inside-out, he picks cultural activities on dates... and now that I think of it, he spent a lot of time talking with a man at the museum gift shop."

Sharon's friend interrupts: "Wait. You think he's gay?"

"I don't know. What do you think?" asks Sharon.

"I don't think so but who knows, you know? Maybe he's just European. They tend to be way more cultured and dress different, better," says her friend. "Has he made a move yet?"

"He's kissed me many times. He tried to invite himself up the other night but it felt too soon, so I stalled."

"Maybe you should let him up to find out," jokes her friend.

"Maybe," says Sharon, a huge knot forming in her stomach.

Feeling uneasy, Sharon decides to call Angelo and invite him out for coffee. Maybe seeing him again will make her feel better and answer some lingering questions. Her cell reception lousy at home, she looks up the number and calls Angelo from her landline. He answers but this time his accent is mysteriously missing.

"Angelo?" asks Sharon.

"Yeah, you got him" he says.

"Hi. This is Sharon." The silence that follows is stifling.

"Hi Sharon," says Angelo, his accent suddenly resurfacing, "How are you bella?"

"I'm fine. I was thinking about you and hoping you were free later. Want to meet for coffee?"

Angelo agrees and the date's set for that evening but Sharon can't believe what's just happened. *Did she imagine it? Did he not recognize her phone number and answer without an accent? Weren't accents permanent?* God knows, the French man three cubicles down at work had been attending accent reduction classes for at least 5-months with little improvement.

At coffee, Sharon asks more about Angelo's work and his passion for science. She can tell he genuinely loves what he does; she just can't tell if *he's* genuine. Angelo mentions his visa and how he's afraid it will expire soon.

"Soon?" asks Sharon. "I thought you recently arrived."

At this, she notices Angelo's expression changes. He takes a sip of his coffee then says "I know right? It shouldn't be this way but Americans are so tough with their visa requirements. And P visas have all these rules."

"P visas?" asks Sharon.

"Yes, professors get a P visa. So silly, P for professor equals P visa."

At this Sharon laughs and thinks to herself, *he really is charming,* but then, about 30-minutes into the date she isn't so charmed anymore.

"Sharon, I didn't want to skip our meeting but I really have to go. I have to meet with a student in preparation for tomorrow," says Angelo, standing up and giving her a perfunctory hug with a pat on the back.

Head down, shoes heavy, Sharon walks home upset, wondering what she did wrong. She thinks this is goodbye. It hasn't occurred to her that Angelo is likely skipping out because of what she did right. He's a con artist but Sharon hasn't quite connected the dots just yet.

Let's recap:

First of all, there are more than 20 nonimmigrant visa types for people traveling to the United States on a temporary-basis. There are many more types of immigrant visas for people coming to live in the United States permanently. The type of visa you need is determined by the purpose of your travel. There is such a thing as a P visa but it's not for professors, it's for performing athletes, artists, and entertainers. For full information on visas, visit: www.travel.state.gov/visa. Here you may learn the different types of available visas, their requirements, and even how to accurately read visa documentation.

The one thing you won't find out—if a person has a visa. Under U.S. law, specifically the Immigration and Nationality Act (INA) 222(f), visa records are confidential.

If you want to know if a person is an illegal immigrant, you can only do so if you are verifying for employment purposes. Since U.S. law requires companies to employ only individuals who may legally work in the United States, only U.S. citizens and foreign citizens who have the necessary authorization may legally work in America. As a result, E-Verify (www.dhs.gov/e-verify) allows businesses to determine the eligibility of their employees to work in the United States. The online database is free for employers and non-profits.

In Sharon's case, this won't help but what will help is looking up the visa types and realizing that a P visa isn't for professors. Since Angelo hammered home that P was for professors, it's safe to say that he was lying—at the very least about his visa status.

But what about his mysteriously disappearing accent? Was Angelo really Italian? Yes and no. Turns out, Angelo was Italian-American. When Sharon later entered his name into Zabasearch.com she found a series of New York addresses. He was a life-long New Yorker who grew up in Little Italy and now lived nearby. His accent was convenient, he used it to seduce women, like Sharon, who instantly fell for his charm.

While Angelo was fluent in Italian, if she were unsure she could have called the LanguageLine.com at 1-800-752-6096. Here she'd be able to pay to have a phone conversation with the help of a language interpreter. This way she could verify Angelo truly spoke Italian and wasn't merely whispering sweet nothings into her ear.

And what about his sexuality? Well, that's a tad trickier to decipher.

"If somebody's gay and wants to hide it it's hard to tell," explains Jordan Harbinger, co-founder of The Art of Charm, a Los Angeles-based company that teaches men advanced social skills and dating science.

"You can look for stereotypical things like effeminate voice and mannerisms but those aren't a tell-tale sign. There are guys that have religious or sheltered backgrounds and that's just the way they are," says Harbinger.

"Look for ambiguous signs of past relationships," he says. Heterosexual and metrosexual men are still going to be touching [women] and taking things to the next level but most men are scared of rejection, which can affect how they act on a date."

"It's important to take the clues in combination," reminds Harbinger, who runs a residential week-long training program that accepts six men at a time at a man pad in Hollywood, California. Five instructors take turns teaching the men about elements of body language, vocality, tonality, eye contact, confidence, and how to respond in high-pressure situations. For details check out TheArtOfCharm.com

In the end, whether Angelo was gay or straight, Italian or not, in the U.S. permanently or on a visa, he wasn't the right match for Sharon. He was also dishonest and disingenuous. She may be disappointed today that things didn't work out but in the long run it's for the best.

What's that Italian-American expression? *Arrivederci sucker!*

If only it were that easy for Jane. At 39, she's decided to venture into the world of online dating, despite the stern warning against it from her overbearing mother. And why not? Jane is determined to put herself out there and gauge her possibilities.

Attractive, smart, and outgoing, Jane is still unable to shake her mom's disapproving words out of her head. So, she opts to online date for free as a test drive. This way she won't waste any money if her mom ends up being right when she says that only scam artists date online via personal ads.

After various fun and interesting dates using PlentyofFish.com and posting ads on Craigslist.org, Jane decides to go mainstream and pays to join a dating site. Two-weeks in she's pleased with the results... she hasn't met the man of her dreams but she feels she's inching closer and she's having a good time along the way. Then, one day she logs in to find she has an email from Brad, a 45-year-old divorced Bay Area architect who lives in her same zip code and shares her love of sailing. Jane is overjoyed.

After a few email exchanges and a phone call, Brad invites Jane out for drinks at a cozy, upscale, bar on a Wednesday. He's everything she thought he'd be. Her heart's racing and she's hoping this date will end with the promise of another. She doesn't have to wait long. Less than 40-minutes into their first meeting, Brad's already arranged for another date this Friday and one more on Sunday afternoon. Jane is thrilled to be out with a successful career man, who takes the lead, and isn't busy playing games.

That night, Jane drove herself home. About 20-minutes after she'd arrived at her apartment, Brad texted to make sure she got home alright. She went to bed happy and looking forward to Friday.

The next day at work, Brad texted several times. In the evening he texted several more and when Jane got caught up cooking dinner for some girlfriends, Brad called to see why he hadn't heard from her. At first, Jane was flattered. What a problem to have, a great guy who's interested in her day! She felt lucky, fortunate, to have someone so fully vested in her life—and off the bat, to boot.

But by Friday, Jane had to make sure her phone was on silent at work. Brad was texting non-stop. What was once welcome interest now started to feel controlling. Despite this, Jane wasn't used to such straight-forward men and this non-game playing approach intrigued her.

That night, sitting beside Brad at an elegant restaurant he leaned in and told her he loved her. Jane gasped. She was taken aback. *Love? It's our second date,* she thought... but who was she to discourage the love of such a worthy man? *Maybe this is how grown-ups date,* she told herself.

Having agreed to arrive at the restaurant together, Jane accepted a ride home from Brad. As she buckled her seatbelt, she noticed Brad backed out of the parking spot rather quickly. As she shrugged it off she couldn't hide her body tensing up again as he raced through a yellow light, a split-second before it turned red. Brad noticed her reaction and laughed, "I'm an excellent driver," he assured her.

At home, Brad walked Jane to her apartment door. She didn't invite him in and he didn't ask, but he did confirm their date for Sunday. As Jane entered her apartment she felt uncomfortable but didn't quite know why. She went over the events of her day and called a friend to chat.

A few minutes into her call she gets a beep from an incoming call on the other line, and notices it is Brad. Let's listen as she puts her friend on hold and switches over.

"What are you doing?" Brad asks.

"I'm on the other line with a friend. Is everything OK?

"A woman friend or a guy friend?" Brad asks.

Jane doesn't like this. "Just a friend," she says. "Call me when you get home, I need to click back."

Jane's worried. Is Brad moving too fast? What's with the constant communication? All her life she'd wanted an attentive man, but not *this* attentive.

Not even 15-minutes later, Brad calls again.

"Home so soon?" asks Jane.

"Nah, 10-more minutes to go but I missed you," says Brad.

"Ah, I'm flattered but I'm still on the other line. I'll call you later," says Jane

"When, later?" asks Brad.

"I don't know Brad, when I finish talking with my friend."

"Fine," huffs Brad, before hanging up.

Annoyed, Jane finishes her talk with her friend and then powers off her cell phone.

The next day she had eight voicemail messages from Brad. She decided right then and there to end it. Prince Charming had turned into a nightmare. His behavior seemed controlling of her and at the same time, uncontrollable.

Was Jane too quick to judge? It doesn't matter. Only Jane's opinion is what counts. Her uneasiness was palpable. It was her job to take care of herself.

Let's look at the signs. Perhaps she was on to something.

Remember Brad's speedy confession to love? He's a racecar lover. These speed devils can spell real danger. In fact, Investigation Discovery has a television show called *Who the (Bleep) Did I Marry?* in which many of the women married criminals who were quick to profess feelings of deep love and/or show overwhelming affection.

Another sign of incompatibility was Brad's driving.

"If the man does not change his way of driving because of the passenger that's a big indication of his character," says Dr. Leon James, psychology professor at the University of Hawaii who has written books and articles on driving psychology alongside his wife, Dr. Diane Nahl.

"If she's in the car and he drives his usual way or tries to show off taking risks and she's worried or scared and he's not accommodating, he's not going to accommodate to what she wants later either."

Dr. James says there's a direct correlation between how a person drives and their overall behavior in times of conflict. "If he's going to be self-centered behind the wheel, he will be self-centered as a boyfriend, as a lover, as a husband to his wife." Dr. James's site, DrDriving.org, is a great tool that's fully-loaded with useful facts on the psychology of driving, traffic and road rage.

But road trip aside, what about Brad's constant

phone calls and wanting to know how Jane's day went? That doesn't seem so self-centered. Oh, but it is. Brad's behavior from the get-go was domineering, over-powering, and overwhelming. He set up two additional dates, less than an hour into the first one. On their second date, he'd professed feelings of love. His constant texts may have been flattering at first but they quickly crossed a line into inappropriate, even though the messages weren't inherently so.

Jane may want to block Brad from calling her mobile phone. Wireless retailer, Wirefly, put together some great step-by-step instructions on how to block unwanted wireless calls to your cell phone at: www.wirefly.com/learn/how-to/how-to-block-unwanted-calls-to-your-cell-phone. Technology constantly changing, if you need something more specific, try performing an Internet search for *your service provider, type of phone and block calls* to make sure you get the most up-to-date information.

If Jane had been unsure if Brad's phone behavior was out of line by societal standards, she could have downloaded an app that educates people on digital dating abuse. The app is for iPhone and was originally created to help parents of teenagers understand what their grown child may be experiencing when dealing with digital abuse but it is also an excellent tutorial for all adults and provides various links to additional resources. It may be downloaded free at Loveisnotabuse.com or at the iTunes store.

Thirty-year-old Hannah isn't as lucky. She's been dating her co-worker, Clyde, for more than a month and is finally invited over to his apartment to watch a movie next Friday. Excited to get to know Clyde better, Hannah spends the week picking out the perfect outfit. These past few months have been a whirlwind and while she feels she knows Clyde well, she's guarded as she doesn't want her peers to know of her office romance. She also can't wait to get to see Clyde's home and hear him play his guitar. Clyde has said many times that he auditioned for various successful bands and was often a final candidate to play bass.

As planned, Clyde leaves work around 5:30 pm on Friday and Hannah stays till nearly 7 pm when she unfolds the piece of paper Clyde slipped her during the day with the address to his place. She is taken aback to find the words "call me," but picks up the phone to call.

Let's listen in.

"Hi, Clyde, this is Hannah."

"Hey Hannah, you heading over?" asks Clyde.

"Well, I'd like to but there isn't an address to your apartment in the piece of paper you gave to me earlier. What's up with that?"

"Oh, I just wanted a heads up so I could tidy a few things around the place," says Clyde.

Hannah shrugs it off. Makes sense, she thinks. "Well, um, where do I go?"

After jotting down the address and scribbling directions, Hannah's on her way. Forty-minutes later she rings the buzzer to Clyde's apartment complex and is let into a hallway. As she's about to knock on Clyde's door he opens it and tells her to "stand still."

"What?" asks Hannah.

"Hold it. Just hold it right there one second," says Clyde, as he bends down to put blue hospital-like footies over Hannah's shoes.

"Clyde, what are you doing?" asks Hannah.

"It's very germy out there," he says. "I keep everything germ-free."

Uneasy, Hannah jokes "Am I sterile now?"

"Almost," says Clyde, pouring a large amount of sanitizer onto her hands. "There," he says.

Then, "Cell phone, please."

"You must be kidding!" says Hannah.

"I want to sanitize it. Do you know how many bacteria live in your phone?"

Hannah rolls her eyes. "Clyde, you're not drenching my cell phone in sanitizer."

Now in a bad mood, Hannah walks in to the apartment and notices Clyde has only just unpacked. How can this be? He's lived in the area, in this apartment, for several years. She surveys the room—not a single photograph, nothing personal, just a few cardboard boxes, some of which are hidden with a throw, and a rackety bookshelf loaded with books on physics and science. In the corner she spots a guitar.

"Hey, before it gets too late play me a song on your guitar," says Hannah.

"Well, I was hoping we could eat first. I'm hungry."

"Great, where are we going?" asks Hannah, who doesn't really know how to cook. By the looks of the place- no kitchen table, no chairs- she imagines neither does Clyde.

"I picked up some pizza when you called that you were on your way. By the way, does anyone know you're here?" asks Clyde.

Now, Hannah imagines Clyde meant did anyone at work know she was there, but there's something about the way he asks the question that gives her a bad feeling in the pit of her stomach.

"Just my girlfriends," says Hannah.

"You told them my address?"

"I told them I was meeting you," says Hannah, skirting the question.

"What if they tell someone where I live?" asks Clyde, his voice now louder, slightly stern.

"Why would they tell anyone where you live?" asks Hannah, as Clyde paces into the other room.

"Your pizza, miss," he says as he hands her a slice on a paper plate.

Curious, Hannah walks into the other room. Clyde only has two slices total—one for Hannah and one for himself. Hannah finds this weird. *Who invites you over for dinner and only has one slice of pizza for you to eat?*

"Thanks, um, do you mind if I use the restroom real quick? I want to wash my hands. I know they're

sanitized and all but nothing beats good old-fashioned soap."

In the bathroom Hannah reaches for the soap but finds dishwashing detergent. The water is ice cold. She begins to look around and notices there is no toilet paper, only some colored napkins from a fast food joint. Hannah's gone from excited to eager to leave.

She exits the bathroom to find Clyde on his bed watching a video.

"Can you grab us some drinks?" he asks.

Hannah opens the fridge and grabs a beer for Clyde and a soda for herself. She reaches in the cupboard to find a glass but instead finds several rolls of half-used duct tape and absolutely nothing else. Hannah freezes. She's suddenly terrified. She replays the scenario in her head: germaphobe, no one knows where she is, no real soap, no toilet paper. Her breathing changes. She thinks back to the news and the story of Laci Peterson who was killed by her husband and how he had duct tape in his car, presumably to use with his next victim.

"Hey Hannah, what's taking so long?" hollers Clyde.

"Clyde, I just realized I have to go. I'm really sorry. I thought I could stay but I just realized I can't, I have a very early work commitment tomorrow."

As Hannah heads to the door, Clyde runs up behind her.

"Don't leave, Hannah, you just got here. Stay a while at least."

"I really want to but I can't," says Hannah, reaching for her handbag. Clyde snatches it and holds it to his chest.

"Cute, Clyde but I need my purse. I really have to go."

"Why? Why do you have to go?" demands Clyde. She can tell his breathing is changing too.

"I told you. I forgot I have a very early day tomorrow and I need to leave now."

Thinking: to hell with my stuff, just get me out of here, Hannah turns to slightly face the door and notices five dead bolt locks. In her peripheral vision she notices that there are metal bars on all the windows of his is a ground level apartment.

"Clyde, please open the door."

"No," says Clyde.

"Clyde, please open the door. I have to go."

"No," repeats Clyde.

"Clyde, please open the door. I have to go," says Hannah, feeling her legs start to shake. It takes about four more requests before Clyde opens the Jenga puzzle that comprises the door.

"Here," says Clyde, tossing Hannah her handbag. *"We're over!"*

Hannah could care less. The second he opens the door she makes a run for it. She catches her bag in midair. Freaked out, she doesn't go home. She goes to stay with a friend. But Hannah's ordeal is far from over.

The next day at work, Clyde keeps calling her line to ask what had happened. He begs her to meet afterward. Desperate to get him off her case, Hannah agrees to meet at a coffee shop around the corner for 10-minutes after work. There things escalate. Clyde tells her he'll go straight to their boss and accuse her of harassment if she refuses to see him again.

Hannah knows her job is on the line. Her workplace has a strict policy against personal relationships of this nature.

That night, she drives home scared.

Over the next week, Hannah receives threatening messages from Clyde. She wants to go to the police but she doesn't want to make this into a bigger deal. She just wants it to go away. Fortunately it does--when his messages go unanswered, Clyde switches his attention to another co-worker who files a harassment complaint, which eventually leads to Clyde's termination.

Hannah was very lucky. We can't know for sure if Clyde had any intent to physically harm her but it sure didn't look good. She did the right thing by getting out of there as quickly as possible.

"We stop being uncomfortable when we distance ourselves from that which is causing the discomfort," explains Joe Navarro, a 25 year veteran of the FBI and the author of *What Every Body is Saying* as well as *Louder Than Words*. Navarro, who made a living studying body language and catching criminals says our bodies are key indicators of our feelings and those of others.

But what about Hannah's broken-record approach in demanding that Clyde open the door? Was that the best tactic?

Probably not, but it worked.

Alex Yaroslavsky a conflict resolution expert in New York City, suggests a different escape plan.

"Fake a stomach ache, go into a bathroom and call a friend," he suggests, explaining these one-on-one date situations can be very tricky. "Most people who are daters are not professional psychologists or conflict resolvers or hostage negotiators," he empathizes.

Like Navarro, Yaroslavsky recommends you remove yourself from the situation as quickly as possible: "When you're creeped out in this situation... it is not unlike a hostage negotiator where you have to befriend the person. Your job is to make them like you in some way. You have to make them trust you. I know, when the blood drains away from your face the last thing you're thinking about is trust but come up with something innocent, come back with a beer and fake a stomach ache," he says.

"Whatever you do, don't say things like 'you're crazy' or 'you're weird,' that will only make the person defensive."

So when *do* you call the police? "When you feel physically in danger, that's what the police is there for you," instructs Yaroslavsky.

Despite the things learned in retrospect, there were clues Hannah could have picked up along the way: Clyde didn't seem to have work friends. Once inside his apartment his lack of furniture, hot water, toilet paper, and "live in" coziness were all signs something was amiss. It wasn't enough to know what was what, but it was enough to know to proceed with caution.

Upon further probing, Hannah might have learned that Clyde lived on food stamps, was facing eviction, and was a kleptomaniac who often stole food from supermarket shelves. He wore his coat all year long so that he could have a place to hide stolen items. Interestingly enough, food stamps don't buy toilet paper, which probably explains why Clyde had napkins from fast food chains in his chilly bathroom.

Though perhaps, the first warning sign came before Hannah even arrived at Clyde's house. Remember the note that was supposed to hold his home address? Clyde didn't want his address scribbled anywhere in advance. It's what he *didn't* want communicated that was the most telling.

People who have nothing to hide, hide nothing.

Oh, alma mater

LIBERAL ARTS SCHOOLS churn out Liberal Arts students. Business schools graduate business students. Each school has a different mission and caters to different skill sets and interests. Where your date went to school and what she or he studied (or didn't study) are valuable pieces of information.

Megan is just about to find this out. She's on a date with Daniel, a 27-year old investment banker, who is alert, savvy, and highly educated. The Harvard-graduate has 26-year-old Megan in the palm of his hand. This is their fourth date.

"Tell me more about life at Harvard," says Megan. "Is it really as tough as it seems in movies or is that just a lot of hype?"

"It's even more challenging," says Daniel. "Classes are long and while the subjects are interesting some of the professors are rather dry. There was one class

where I could hear the clock ticking."

Megan laughs. "Did your professors always wear suits?"

"Sometimes," says Daniel. "What about your college? What was Brown like?" he asks.

"It was great but more of a regular college experience, I guess. It had your usual core classes. I did take an elective in urban archaeology and got to help with fieldwork near a church; that was a lot of fun."

"Brown is in Rhode Island, right?" asks Daniel.

"Providence," confirms Megan.

"Urbana wasn't great but it was close to home," says Daniel.

"Oh, what's in Illinois?" asks Megan, trying to pile her lettuce and tomato onto her fork.

"Urbana?" utters Daniel, looking confused.

" Urbana," replies Megan. "Didn't you just say Urbana was close to home?"

"Oh, right," says Daniel, sipping his water. "I did my first year of college at Northwestern then transferred to Harvard. My grades weren't quite there and I was told I needed to boost my GPA and reapply. Plus it was so much closer to Decatur, it helped me to save some money."

Megan smiles. Daniel is smart, sexy, and ambitious.

The following week, Daniel phones Megan and sets

up a date for a quick drink that night. He says something important has come up and he'd like to discuss it with her.

Megan agrees but when she hangs up the phone, she's nervous. *Could there be somebody else? What's so suddenly urgent*, she wonders. Still, she brushes the thoughts aside. Their last date went very well and nothing negative has happened since. She decides to wait the five or six hours and rein in her imagination.

At 5:30 pm, Megan leaves work for a quiet coffee shop on the other side of Connecticut, about a 30-minute drive from work. She arrives just after 6 pm and finds Daniel sitting in a corner. He stands to greet her and kisses her hello, takes her coat. Megan is relieved. Let's listen...

"You look beautiful," he says.

"Thanks," she blushes.

"I ordered you an espresso," he says. "I even had the barista add some cinnamon," a big smile spreading across his face.

"Perfect," says Megan. "I love cinnamon." She takes a sip and sits down. "So, what's this important news of yours? Are we celebrating something?" asks Megan.

"Maybe," says Daniel. "But if we do, I'd like us to both capitalize."

"Capitalize?" asks Megan, leaning forward. "How so?"

"Well," starts Daniel. "I have this new investment opportunity. It's a slam dunk, win-win. I just had to tell somebody and not just anybody. I can't have people knowing about it but it could make me a ton of money,

nearly a 40-percent return in like, no time."

Megan listens carefully. Daniel is so passionate. His grey eyes look fantastic against the black henley he is wearing today. The details become a blur. As Daniel speaks, she envisions what she could buy with her new investment return. She thinks her parents would be so happy... she could fly home more frequently to visit and the idea of such financial freedom, she has to admit, is wonderful.

"How much would I need to invest?" asks Megan.

"Well it's up to you really," says Daniel. "The more you invest the bigger the return and we are talking almost doubling your money in a few months," he reminds her.

"Forty-percent, you estimate?"

"Yes," nods Daniel. "But again, it's not something you should be sharing with anyone unless you trust they would keep it quiet. If they want to invest too, that's fine, as long as they're a good friend of yours."

"All I really have in savings is shy of $5,000," confides Megan. "I wouldn't want to risk all of it."

"The risk is minimal," says Daniel. "Plus you'll be nearly doubling it while you sleep."

"Still," says Megan. "I'd rather invest a little at first and see how it goes and if it nearly doubles, then that's double the amount I can invest down the line," she says. "I can put in $1,000."

"A thousand? Great. You sure you don't want to put in

*$2,000 and get nearly $4,000 back in a few months,"
asks Daniel.*

*Megan thinks about it a bit longer, has a sip of her
cinnamon-covered espresso. "OK, I'll meet you half
way, Daniel. $1,500. You drive a hard bargain," she
laughs.*

*"Terrific," says Daniel. "I'll need a cashier's check in my
name first thing. What time's your bank open?"*

*"I think it's still open now," says Megan. "It closes late
on Wednesday."*

*"Oh you're TD Bank?" asks Daniel. "What luck! There's
a TD Bank right around the corner from here."*

"Great! Let's go," says Megan, reaching for her coat.

That was the last time Megan ever saw Daniel or
her $1,500.

It pays to get familiar with locations. Daniel's hiccup
over dinner on their fourth date should've set off a red
flag in Megan's mind—but she was too consumed with her
intelligent and sexy date for it to register.

Harvard is in Cambridge, Massachusetts, not in
Illinois. Megan came close to this fleeting realization.
Another flag—Decatur, Illinois, is more than a 2-hour drive
to Evanston, Illinois, where Northwestern University is
located. It's unrealistic that Daniel would drive two-hours
each way to school, that's 4-hours round trip every day
(longer in snow), especially when he made a comment
that hinted he needed to be careful with finances at that
time.

From the get-go, Daniel talked up Harvard and insisted he graduated from there. Megan could've called the registrar's office and tried to verify if this were true. If she had a friend who worked in the human resources field, she could have paid the nominal fee for a degree check through Web sites specifically created for this purpose (e.g. www.studentclearinghouse.org) for recruiters, headhunters, and corporations to use. Lastly, Megan could also have looked to see what colleges and universities were in Urbana, in or near Decatur, and if it were important enough to her, she could have called to see if Daniel went to college there and if he ever transferred out.

Other ways to verify college attendance, not necessarily graduation, include alumni magazines, online announcements, and past information on student groups. Sometimes if a Web site no longer has the information you're looking for, the WayBackMachine can help. Turn to www.Archive.org and enter the Web site into the WayBackMachine and click on "take me back," to search old Web pages. The site, known as the Internet Archive, is a non-profit that's building a digital library of Internet sites and other cultural artifacts in digital form. The service is free.

And who's to say Daniel is in finance at all? Did Megan call the switchboard where Daniel works and dial by name or ask to be transferred to his extension? So far, all Megan's clued in on is that Daniel's alert. She's right, he is smart. He is also manipulative and several steps ahead of her. Remember, it was Daniel's last-minute suggestion that Megan drive 30-minutes out of her way to a coffee shop around the corner from a branch of her bank. Daniel also convinced Megan to invest money without asking for more information. He then established intimacy, expressing this was a private investment but if she wanted to tell a good friend or two, who wouldn't blab, that would be okay. Daniel is a con artist—and a very good one.

But is he an investment banker too? Well, for that the North American Securities Administrators Association (NASAA) could shed some light. State securities regulators have been protecting investors for more than 100 years from fraud.

Every state has a securities administrator that is responsible for the Daniels of the world. In other words, the securities administrator in your state is responsible for licensing broker-dealers and investment advisers, registering certain securities offerings, reviewing financial offerings of small companies, auditing branch office sales practices and record-keeping, promoting investor education, and enforcing state securities laws, among other obligations.

The NASAA's Web site would've been a good place for Megan to start. From there, she'd likely be referred to The Financial Industry Regulatory Authority (FINRA), the largest independent regulator for all securities firms doing business in the United States. Megan could've called FINRA's BrokerCheck Hotline at (800) 289-9999 to get Daniel's Central Registry Deposit (CRD) number, which is his broker's license number. She could also perform a free broker check at www.finra.org/Investors/ToolsCalculators/BrokerCheck.

The CRD is a computerized database that will tell you a stockbroker's employment history (dating back to 1997, when the database was created), securities examination scores, licensing or registration status, and disciplinary history.

As an investor, Megan could request a public report of background information on any stockbroker or brokerage firm. Depending on state jurisdiction, this report may be free or obtained for a nominal fee. Megan is lucky that Daniel disappeared from her life instantly—and that he only took $1,500.

If Megan were like most of us, she would have confided her great deal in a friend. She would have gone on and on about how fantastic and smart Daniel was. There's no greater advertising than word-of-mouth. There's a high probability Megan's friend would have invested money too. She trusts Megan. Megan trusts Daniel. The cycle perpetuates based on good intent but you end up with a close-knit circle of friends, scammed inadvertently, by each other! This is an affinity scam, the exact type of scam the NASAA has been warning daters and social media users about for a while.

People like Daniel cozy up to someone or worm their way into a group of friends. It could be via Facebook where people tend to accept as "friends" people who are connected via someone they know. One person could have five people in common and not know a soul. It's important to pick up the phone and ask your real friends how they know the people within their circles, particularly when money is at stake.

Another flag—this one with flying colors—is that Daniel demanded a cashier's check in his name. Reputable transactions have reputable records. If you are asked for a cashier's check in the name of a broker, it should sound an alarm in your head.

Before you invest—sleep on it. Where's the fire? What's so urgent it has to be this nanosecond? Nothing.

Not when your life savings are concerned—whether that's $1 or $1M. If you earned it, it's yours to keep until you decide otherwise.

Ask for details. Look up the company at www.finance.yahoo.com (for free) or hoovers.com (for a fee). Who are the executives? Who's on the board? How long has it been around? It is a private or public company? Does it trade—at what price? Has the stock changed drastically lately? Why? Ask. Ask. Ask.

Make sure you look for the company's financial statements on the U.S. Securities and Exchange Commission (SEC) Web site at www.sec.gov/edgar/searchedgar/companysearch.html. Company filings are available dating back to 1994. You want to make sure you are looking at the U.S. SEC, not something that says the Bahamas or elsewhere.

And lastly, Megan should have asked for her deal In writing. Regardless of whom you're in business with, make sure you obtain a prospectus; ask for written documentation that details the risks of the investment and lists the procedures for how to get your money out.

Deal or no deal, Megan should also have found a polite way to decline the espresso. She wasn't there when Daniel ordered it and has no way of knowing if any type of drug was put into her drink. While no one wants to presume the worst of their date—in the getting to know someone process, trust needs to earned and that's an investment of time.

"In terms of the long term success of a relationship you really want to put less attention on the personality match," explains Arthur Aron, a social psychologist at

Stonybrook University. "What's very important is that values match but put attention on the mental health of your partner. And if you yourself are anxious and depressed the most important thing you can do is to get yourself in therapy."

Arthur Aron has created a set of 36 questions that help you speed up the get-to-know-you process and generate closeness. He calls his questions Fast Friends, though they're also frequently referred to as The Sharing Game. In one hour, Aron's 36 questions, can lead you to a new level of intimacy.

Below are Arthur Aron's 36 questions from the Personality & Social Psychology Bulletin by SOCIETY FOR PERSONALITY AND SOCIAL PSYCHOLOGY. Reproduced with permission of SAGE PUBLICATIONS, INC. in the format Journal via Copyright Clearance Center.

1.   Given the choice of anyone in the world, whom would you want as a dinner guest?

2.   Would you like to be famous? In what way?

3.   Before making a telephone call, do you ever rehearse what you are going to say? Why?

4.   What would constitute a "perfect" day for you?

5.   When did you last sing to yourself? To someone else?

6.   If you were able to live to the age of 90 and retain either the mind or body of a 30-year-old for the last 60 years of your life, which would you want?

7.   Do you have a secret hunch about how you will die?

8.   Name three things you and your partner appear to

have in common.

9. For what in your life do you feel most grateful?

10. If you could change anything about the way you were raised, what would it be?

11. Take 4 minutes and tell your partner your life story in as much detail as possible.

12. If you could wake up tomorrow having gained any one quality or ability, what would it be?

13. If a crystal ball could tell you the truth about yourself, your life, the future, or anything else, what would you want to know?

14. Is there something that you've dreamed of doing for a long time? Why haven't you done it?

15. What is the greatest accomplishment of your life?

16. What do you value most in a friendship?

17. What is your most treasured memory?

18. What is your most terrible memory?

19. If you knew that in one year you would die suddenly, would you change anything about the way you are now living? Why?

20. What does friendship mean to you?

21. What roles do love and affection play in your life?

22. Alternate sharing something you consider a positive characteristic of your partner. Share a total of 5 items.

23. How close and warm is your family? Do you feel your childhood was happier than most other people's?

24. How do you feel about your relationship with your mother?

25. Make 3 true "we" statements each. For instance "We are both in this room feeling. . ."

26. Complete this sentence: "I wish I had someone with whom I could share. . . "

27. If you were going to become a close friend with your partner, please share what would be important for him or her to know.

28. Tell your partner what you like about them; be very honest this time saying things that you might not say to someone you've just met.

29. Share with your partner an embarrassing moment in your life.

30. When did you last cry in front of another person? By yourself?

31. Tell your partner something that you like about them already.

32. What, if anything, is too serious to be joked about?

33. If you were to die this evening with no opportunity to communicate with anyone, what would you most regret not having told someone? Why haven't you told them yet?

34. Your house, containing everything you own, catches

fire. After saving your loved ones and pets, you have time to safely make a final dash to save any one item. What would it be? Why?

35. Of all the people in your family, whose death would you find most disturbing? Why?

36. Share a personal problem and ask your partner's advice on how he or she might handle it. Also, ask your partner to reflect back to you how you seem to be feeling about the problem you have chosen.

Arthur Aron's study of interpersonal closeness is described in: Aron, A., Melinat, E., Aron, E. N., Vallone, R. D., & Bator, R. J. The experimental generation of interpersonal closeness: A procedure and some preliminary findings. Personality and Social Psychology Bulletin (23 n4) pp. 374-375, copyright © 1997 by Sage Publications, Inc. Reprinted by Permission of SAGE Publications.

Time is really the only way to get to know anybody better.

It's not just men who blindside women. Many-a-lady has done it too. Ask Robert, he knows all about this.

Robert worked hard in school. He now works at a top notch financial firm in Washington D.C. and spends most of his time buried in The Wall Street Journal. He's smitten when a co-worker introduces him to the Vice President's new Executive Assistant, Monica—prim, proper and whip-smart, she's also exotically beautiful and an animal activist. She seems too good to be true.

Now on his fourth date with Monica, he continues to feel uneasy but he's not sure why. He shrugs it off, remembering he's rather out of practice. Plus, he can't stop hearing his mother's incessant questioning: *Why is it always something? Can't you be happy for once?* He decides to go with the flow.

"I bought this new skirt today," says Monica, holding up her new purchase with pride. "What do you think?"

"It's beautiful," says Robert, reaching out to touch the soft, silky, material.

"I also got this," Monica pulls a fur wrap out of a Nordstrom bag.

"Is that real fur?" asks Robert.

"Um, I'm not sure," says Monica.

"You don't know?" asks Robert, his forehead wrinkles.

"It cost enough to be real fur," jokes Monica.

"I thought you were a big animal activist."

"Of course I'm anti-fur. I was just kidding, of course it's not real," says Monica, tucking both of her new buys into the bag.

Displeased, Robert changes the topic.

"Would you like to come with me to Libby's baby shower this weekend?" asks Robert.

"Who will be there?" asks Monica.

"Um, well, Libby, and a few gals from the office I guess," says Robert. "A few of the office guys say they're going too."

"I have plans this weekend," says Monica. "How about we meet after?"

Robert laughs, "I haven't told you what day it is yet, silly."

"I'm busy both days," snaps Monica. "But I'm free in the evenings."

Robert doesn't like this. "Let me see how tired I am after the shower," he says.

Perplexed and annoyed, Robert drives home. That night, he can't sleep. *What's the deal with Monica? Why did she ask who would be at the shower?* As midnight rolls around he texts his friend and co-worker, James, to ask if he's still up. James calls Robert right away.

"What's up?" asks James. "Are you still sweating over your presentation earlier?

"Hi James," says Robert. "No, that's not it. It's Monica. I can't figure her out."

James laughs "That's just women! Half the time I have no idea what Leslie is talking about. Just nod."

"Have you ever seen her go to lunch with the other women at work?" asks Robert.

"No, now that you mention it but I'm also not really looking so I don't know," explains James. "Why?"

"She wanted to know who would be at Libby's baby shower. Don't you think that's weird?" asks Robert.

"Dude, that's just women," laughs James.

The next day at work, Robert notices the same Nordstrom's bag from the day before on the floor by Monica's desk. When he approaches her for his usual, quick, "good morning," she seems even more peculiar.

"I'm taking it back alright," she snaps.

Robert plays dumb, "Taking what back?"

"The wrap! I'm taking the wrap back. Turns out it's real fur."

"OK," says Robert, trying to distance himself.

Back at his desk he can see Monica in a discussion with her boss. She seems upset but he can't hear why. She follows the VP into his office.

Up to his neck in work, Robert isn't sure how long Monica was in with her boss. He walks past her desk later in the day and she's not there. Neither is the Nordstrom's bag; he figures she went to return it. Sure enough, just before 6 pm, Monica puts her hand on Robert's shoulder and says she wants to apologize for her erratic behavior. She invites Robert for a quick dinner that night.

"How was your day?" asks Robert.

"Oh, the usual," replies Monica. "Yours?"

"I was following up on feedback from my presentation, most of it was good or useful, constructive you know? But, um, are you sure you're OK? I saw you walk into your boss's office and you seemed upset. Then I didn't see you for a while."

"Oh, Phil can be difficult," says Monica. "I also went to return the wrap and drop some stuff off at home."

"Phil?" asks Robert, horrified that Monica refers to her boss with such little respect. Not Mr. Isen, not Phillip but Phil?

"Yeah, the minute he doesn't get his way he becomes a big baby," laughs Monica.

Uneasy, Robert chuckles, for a lack of anything else to do.

"Robert, stay the night with me?" asks Monica.

Any negative thoughts Robert had about Monica are suddenly out the door. While Monica had stayed at Robert's apartment at least once, she'd never invited him to her place and Robert is itching to see her home.

That night, Robert stays over. He can't believe his luck. He had this beautiful woman, who'd invited him to dinner, ask him back to her place. He feels on Cloud 9; until the alarm clock goes off the next morning.

"Good morning beautiful," he says, kissing her on the cheek.

"Good morning," she smiles.

"How's this work?" he asks, half joking, half hurried. "Mind if I hop in the shower first?"

"Nope, go right ahead," says Monica. Towels are in the closet by the entryway."

Robert stumbles over to the closet and Monica rolls back to sleep. Unsure which closet, he opens the one he thought she meant but there are no towels--just a Nordstrom's bag. *Didn't Monica return this?* he thinks.

Oh, she must've kept the silky skirt. Remembering how it felt he reaches in the bag for another touch. His fingertips meet with fur.

"What's this?" he asks, towering over her, holding up the fur wrap.

"My wrap," she says, sheepishly.

"I thought you told me at dinner last night that you returned it," says Robert.

"I was going to but Phil had a cow," she says.

"Phil? Mr. Isen—Phil Isen? Why would he care if you returned the wrap?" asks Robert.

"Because he gave it to me, Robert. Why do you think?"

"What do you mean?"

"Robert, everyone knows I have a special relationship with Phil. You and I aren't exclusive, don't look so straight-laced."

"Not exclusive is one thing but Mr. Isen? You're having an affair with Mr. Isen? What do you mean everybody knows? James doesn't know."

"Who's James?" asks Monica.

"Never mind," says Robert, as he grabs his clothes, pulls them on, and leaves.

Sometimes there's a reason people aren't well-received. It seems Monica was mostly disliked by her female cohorts. Turns out, she was having an affair with one of their bosses, which led her to land the job in the first place and secure special perks in the office. The women resented her preferential treatment, pricey gifts, and impromptu time off.

Hours later when Robert called James, he was stunned; he too had no idea.

Monica, like Daniel, is a manipulator. She may have genuinely liked Robert but she quickly used him to try to cover her tracks among her peers. She thought if she could divert attention from her boss to Robert, perhaps the office women would like her better but she was smart enough to know attending Libby's baby shower would be a misstep.

If Robert had used LinkedIn.com, he would have found out that Libby and Mr. Isen's wife were friends since they attended the same college together. He could have used the graduation dates to further establish the timeline of their friendship. He could also have deduced that Mrs. Isen would most likely be at Libby's baby shower. In fact, the Facebook invite he never took the time to review would show Mrs. Isen would be in attendance too. Robert picked up that Monica was acting strangely about the shower; he just didn't connect the dots.

In retrospect, it makes sense now that Monica didn't know if the wrap were real or fake since it was a gift from her boss, and probably given to her not long before she met up with Robert.

Sometimes we dress for the part we want. Other times we just deceive the world by the part we play. It's hard to tell in this case, which best describes Monica.

Big brother hearts you

THE INTERNET AND social media can be enemies or allies. If you're the one seeking the information it's a goldmine. If you're trying to hide your information It can be a landmine, full of traps. It's important to learn to watch your step, shield your heart, and use technology in your favor.

Facebook and Twitter are just two of countless Web sites out there aimed to help you share and connect. They're also two of countless Web sites out there which, ironically, cause you accidentally to share (sometimes too much) and inadvertently connect with people you'd rather not. Sarah is about to discover this.

Jim likes Sarah. He's just not sure how much he likes her. He also likes Wynn and Tamara. Sarah doesn't know Jim is simultaneously dating other women but she's aware she and Jim aren't just dating each other exclusively. After all, Jim and Sarah have only been on two dates after meeting on an online dating site, which many will say is too soon for exclusivity. Still, Sarah thinks Jim is great and she'd like to see him more. She is hoping things continue moving forward and is disappointed on a Thursday night when she calls Jim and asks him to join her for drinks after work and he declines because of a legal briefing he must prepare for the next day. Sarah feels rejected but always gracious, she says "maybe next time," wishes him well, and hangs up the phone.

Chris, Sarah's co-worker, can't help but overhear the conversation.

"Hey, not to eavesdrop or anything but you know, these cubicles are so close together and all. Want to join my friends and me at McCormick's? Happy hour goes till 8 tonight."

"Sure," says Sarah, thinking: Chris is pretty cute. I can't believe I didn't notice him before.

Later that night, Sarah heads home and to bed. She's stayed out much later than she expected, the time just seemed to fly by. It's a real stretch to remove her make up and brush her teeth before bed; she doesn't even check her cell phone for any missed messages. Wiped out, she turns off her nightlight and goes to sleep.

The next day at work, she finds her thoughts wandering toward Chris, not Jim; she just hasn't realized it yet. Her cell phone nearly losing its charge, Sarah quickly notices she's missed a call this afternoon from Jim. It's an invitation to go out tonight, now that his legal presentation is out of the way. *Why not?* thinks Sarah, as she picks up her work phone to return the call.

That night, Sarah meets Jim at a small, Thai, restaurant

for dinner. Jim shows up and amid conversations, asks Sarah, about her dog.

But there's a logistical problem. Let's listen in:

"That must be your other date," jokes Sarah.

"Oh, why's that?" asks Jim.

"Well, I don't have a dog," says Sarah.

"Oh, I wonder where I got that crazy idea," says Jim.

Always gracious, Sarah, jumps in: "Well, I've always wanted a dog. I just don't think I'm home enough. I might have mentioned it or something."

"Ahh, I guess that's it." replies Jim. "My bad."

As the night continues, Sarah realizes Jim isn't as mesmerizing as she thought he was. He hasn't done anything wrong, per se, but he's just not as 'amazing' as she thought initially.

Maybe if I ask him about water skiing he'll perk up, she thinks.

"So any plans to test out your new water skis?" asks Sarah.

"Water skis?" asks Jim.

"Mhm."

What water skis?" asks Jim.

"The ones your sister got you a few months ago because of the closeout sale," responds Sarah.

"My sister didn't buy me any skis," says Jim, a little confused.

Sarah realizes it's not Jim's sister who bought skis. It's Chris's sister that bought Chris skis when she noticed a nearby sports shop was going out of business. "Oh my," says Sarah. "I must've had a sip of whatever you had earlier," she laughs.

On the drive home, Jim is talking but Sarah is not really listening, she's lost in her own thoughts. *How'd I end up on a date on a Friday night last-minute?* she wonders. *And with Jim? Why didn't he set this up earlier in the week? And why did he think I had a dog?* Then her stomach sinks a little bit. *Well, why did I think his sister gave him skis?* she asks herself candidly. *I think I was thinking about Chris, not Jim. Still, I don't like this last-minute date. I shouldn't have accepted. Were the other girls busy? Was I Plan B? C? There must be at least one other... and she probably has a dog.*

As the car nears her apartment, Jim spots a parking spot, a rarity in this neighborhood. Let's get back to them as they pull in:

"How about a nightcap," asks Jim.

"Tonight?" asks Sarah, for a lack of a comeback.

"Well, yes. I mean, it's fortuitous that we saw this parking spot and it's still early for a Friday night," he says.

"True," says Sarah, "but it's been a long week and I'm quite tired. Perhaps another night," she says, as she leans in to kiss him goodnight.

As she walked to her door, she watched his car drive away... his New York license plate getting smaller and smaller in the distance.

At home, alone, Sarah logs on to Facebook. She's hoping to see what Chris has been up to tonight. *Maybe he's out somewhere and I could "happen to be in the neighborhood,"* she thinks. No luck. He hasn't posted a word.

And then, without rhyme or reason, Sarah pulls up Jim's Facebook page. She sees a post on his wall at 3:42 pm where a woman named Tamara says "Sorry to cancel last-minute, J! Next time!"

Sarah, shakes her head. She knew it. She wasn't bothered that Jim was seeing other people but she didn't like feeling like a second choice. She also didn't like how Jim's decision to come over was based on whether or not he was able to find easy parking near her apartment. While Sarah liked Jim, she didn't like his effortless approach. She wondered if Tamara was old or new, she couldn't tell from Jim's wall when they became Facebook friends. There was something about how she wrote J instead of Jim that seemed trusting, intimate. Annoying.

In retrospect, it's unclear if Sarah was Jim's second choice. It's certainly possible that Jim had standing plans with Tamara and that he, understandably, didn't want to share with Sarah. It's also highly probable that Jim, in fact, did have to work later than usual but that doesn't rule out other plans. He may not have lied or if he did lie, it seems it was a white lie. All in all, Sarah didn't feel slighted; she just didn't feel important *enough*. In truth, it's also probable that Chris had become Sarah's Plan A, even if she hadn't correlated her thoughts and actions to her feelings. It didn't take long after her date with Jim ended before she was online checking Chris's whereabouts.

Luckily, social media revealed a time discrepancy but it didn't reveal much in this instance. Social media; however, can be a real trap. Depending on your social settings, you may be letting more people in on your whereabouts than you'd like. You friends may unintentionally be letting others in on your wanderings too. For instance, if a friend signs you into a location, now people know where you allegedly are or where you went and with whom. It's easy to forget that your friends can impact your online history. The scary part is, this can affect your life in many other ways.

Moreover, there are all sorts of criminals online. You use social media to connect, they use social media to connect the dots. If someone is looking to rob a home, you could become an easy target—especially if you check in to places using mobile technology. Now the crook knows where you are, that you've just arrived, and probably with whom you're there. In other words, you're not home right now. Your home becomes quite attractive. A quick check on WhitePages.com, ZabaSearch.com, Searchbug. com, and many other directories will quickly reveal your address. Check your settings are set to the maximum strength and remember that any information you put online, regardless of how secure you think it is, runs the risk of being shared.

What about the nagging sensation Sarah was left with in regard to Jim's and Tamara's relationship, or shall we say J's and Tamara's relationship? Is there a way to gauge the timeline? The intensity? Yes and no—it really depends on luck.

In New York State it's possible to pay a parking ticket by visiting New York City On-Line Payment Services at www.nycserv.nyc.gov. To use this site, you'll have to presume the person you're looking up has received a ticket. Given how eager Jim was to invite himself up to Sarah's apartment for the ease of finding a parking spot, it's safe to assume at some point he's gotten a parking ticket—and probably recently since it was on his mind. This puts Sarah at a vantage point.

If Sarah had gone to www.nycserv.nyc.gov and chosen "license plate" in the first drop down menu, she could have entered Jim's license plate number and checked to see if he had any recent parking violations. To do this, all she would need is to remember that license plate number she watched drive off in the distance.

If Jim has recent parking tickets or outstanding payments on traffic violations, she would be able to see when and where those tickets were issued. In reality, had Sarah searched Jim's license plate she would have discovered he had an unpaid $90 fine for parking on October 20th at exactly 4:55 am at 669 Lenox Avenue. If she went back into Facebook and looked at Jim's friends, she would have found Tamara's last name. Typing Tamara's first and last name into Zabasearch.com would have revealed her residential address. Entering the ticket address into Google maps as point A and Tamara's residential address as point B, would show that the addresses are close by; HopStop.com would show they were within walking distance (in fact, Jim would've burned 43 calories on a one-way trek)! It's very likely that Jim spent the night at Tamara's, considering that the parking ticket was issued in the early morning hours.

Sarah was lucky. Finding a ticket means someone first had to receive a ticket, which isn't always the case. Jim may be playing the field but in all fairness, he hasn't tricked Sarah as there is no set agreement. There are many variables that account for an answer and sometimes one tool alone won't yield enough clarity. Don't give up.

As good as a resource may be, it can be hit or miss. Depending on what you're looking for, there may be plenty of others routes to the information. If Zabasearch is a dead end when seeking an address, try WhitePages. com. No luck? Try Searchbug.com. Still stuck? Use Google. Keep looking... if you know Tamara has a brother because of the way she's chosen to display her information on Facebook, for instance, then search for Tamara with her brother's last name. Maybe Tamara is divorced and uses her ex-husband's surname.

If one tool isn't working, figure out why. Let your obstacles guide you to a solution. In this day and age of information, there are plenty of tools to help get you where you need to go.

Drew could definitely use a different perspective to solve his own roadblocks. He's smitten with Kendra. Let's join them as they sit at a popular bar after work. They're having a nice time, but Drew can't help but feel Kendra's looking past him to someone a few barstools back.

"Is everything alright?" asks Drew.

"Fine," says Kendra. "Is this a new shirt? It looks really sharp."

"Thanks. I bought it a few weeks ago. Not to harp on it but I can't help but feel that you're looking over there,"

he says, turning his body away to show the direction. "Would you prefer to sit elsewhere?" he asks.

"No," says Kendra, a bit too pronounced, clearly eager to keep her seat.

"OK," says Drew, feeling perplexed.

As the night goes on, Drew continues to feel more and more uneasy. He notices that whenever he shifts his seat, Kendra rearranges hers. She's also running her fingers along the base of her necklace and frequently touching her hair. At one point, it's just too much and Drew excuses himself to use the restroom. He walks slowly to the back of the bar to the restroom area and is relieved there are two other men waiting in line—he now has time to stand in line and observe the situation.

Drew watches as Kendra pulls at her dress and then hikes it to showcase her calf. She then reaches for her pocketbook and reapplies her lip gloss.

Minutes later, as he leaves the loo, he spots a man talking with Kendra. He watches as she reaches out and touches his arm not once but twice throughout their conversation. At one point, he catches Kendra sticking out her neck, as if keeping watch. She doesn't see him and Drew uses the opportunity to walk around and join the duo from the opposite direction. The man speaking with Kendra notices Drew walking closer but since he doesn't personally know Drew, he disregards him. When Drew walks up and introduces himself, he notices Kendra looks flushed.

"Hi there, I'm Drew," he says.

"Hiya Drew, Steve. I couldn't help but notice the bartender was much quicker over here."

"Is she?" said Drew. "I hadn't noticed," though he does notice the man doesn't have a drink.

"Yeah, took forever waiting over there," confirms Steve.

"Did you drink your drink already?" says Drew, with a nervous laugh.

"Oh, they don't have the vodka I like here," explains Steve.

"What vodka is that?" asks Drew.

"Grey Goose," says Steve.

"Ah, Grey Goose is definitely top shelf."

Seconds later, Steve excuses himself and Drew and Kendra continue with their date.

As the night winds down, Kendra excuses herself to use the ladies room. The bar nearly empty, Drew calls the bartender over and asks her what types of vodka they have—sure enough, Grey Goose is on the menu.

When Kendra returns, she and Drew leave the bar together and walk to their cars, where they part ways.

At home, Drew hits social media in search for answers. He starts on Facebook. Since he's just started to date Kendra, they aren't yet Facebook friends but that doesn't mean he's unable to view her friends. He pulls up her list and types Steve—nothing. Then he types Stephen and up comes the photo of the man at the bar. Drew reaches for a post-it and writes down Steve's full name. Then he clicks on Steve's name and goes to his profile, his settings are a tad more loose than Kendra's, so he's able to view some photos. In Steve's most recent holiday album he notices family members are tagged and he jots down the names of siblings and friends that appear frequently. He clicks and clicks and learns more about Steve—seemingly he grew up in New Jersey, has two sisters, and one brother. His dad collects ships in bottles. Useful? Hard to know yet.

As Drew sits there, trying to piece together the mystery of whether or not Kendra and Steve know each other, he replays the evening in his head. He remembers how quick Kendra was to keep her seat, how her neck stretched over his shoulder when he moved his, and how Steve claimed the bar didn't stock Grey Goose vodka; it was just odd and something about the whole thing bugged him. More than anything, it was the unnecessary lying that drew Drew to seek answers.

Not sure if he's done searching Facebook, Drew opens a new window and goes to LinkedIn. Now that he has Steve's full name, he types it in the search box and up comes his profile. He's about to click on it, when he realizes Steve will likely see this; so he takes a step back. He chooses to first anonymize his LinkedIn settings.

Drew goes to the LinkedIn home page and clicks his name from the upper right hand corner. Then he selects "settings." Once on the account settings page he scrolls down to where it says "privacy controls" and clicks on the third option "select what others see when you've viewed their profile." He then selects: "You will be totally anonymous" and clicks to save and exit. By choosing this anonymous option, Drew has disabled his profile stats, which he likes to leave on so he can see whose viewed his profile for career reasons, so he makes a note on his post-it to remember to switch his settings back once he's done researching.

Now he's ready to click on Steve's profile. He learns Steve went to Arizona State University, which is the same college Kendra went to. He looks at the year Steve received his degree but it's at least 8-years ahead of Kendra's; it's unlikely they met during college but having gone to the same university seems like a big clue.

Mulling over the information, Drew is about to call it a night. Then suddenly he perks up: *Maybe one of the siblings can tie this together*, he thinks.

Drew reaches for his post-it and types in the first sister's name but learns she attended a college in the Midwest. He then searches for the other sister and sees that she graduated from Arizona State a year before Kendra. He wonders if Kendra and Steve's middle sister knew each other at college. He jumps back over to Facebook and types his sister's name but her privacy settings won't allow access to her photos. He wonders if the two gals were friends at school? *Roommates perhaps?* He estimates that Kendra must have had a crush on Steve or have dated him to account for her odd behavior earlier in the evening.

All these possibilities are fine with Drew, after all, he's been in college, he's made friends, had roommates, had crushes, had girlfriends. No big deal. The problem is the cover up—why did Kendra and Steve feel they had to hide that they knew each other? Even if they'd dated, couldn't they just have admitted they were friends, at least? The need to hide something turned the incident into a big deal for Drew.

In the weeks that followed, he returned Kendra's calls and met her for dinner one night, but he still felt uneasy. He wondered if she'd cover up something so small, *what would happen when something bigger came along?* Fully aware that life gets more complicated more often than not, Drew decided to move on, sans Kendra.

Ironically, about two years later he was at a local bar and ran into Kendra, with a sparkling engagement ring and a huge smile on her face. Drew kissed her on the cheek and congratulated her. Asking who the lucky guy was, he was not exactly stunned to learn it was Steve.

Kendra apologized for having acted so skittish that night long ago and explained that Steve was her friend's big brother and she'd always had a crush on him. She had just learned a few weeks prior to her date with Drew that Steve was back in town and she hadn't expected to run into him that night. It took another three months for Steve to call her; he said he was nervous to date his sister's friend, said Kendra, gushing and rolling her eyes.

Drew congratulated Kendra and continued toward the back of the bar where he spotted his friends. As the night progressed he noticed somehow they'd ended up near the front again, and his friends and Kendra's had intermingled. A pretty blonde came up and started talking with Drew's group. She was funny- really funny, and soon had everyone in stitches. He felt as if he knew her, *but from where?* Then he realized the woman was Steve's sister and Kendra's college friend. Drew smiled thinking of an opening line, then seemingly out of nowhere he thought: *go Sun Devils.*

Walk the talk

SOMETIMES MEN AND women flat out lie. The dominatrix who's not ready to reveal her day job becomes a gal Friday, (after all, that's how she was lured to the job); the surgeon who performed the procedure may have his medical license under scrutiny; the alleged pilot with a double-life may be scared of heights. So how do you know if your date is really employed in the business he or she claims to be? And how do you know this person is on the up and up? If the economy has taught us anything, it's that there's a difference between being unemployed and being unemployable. And if life can remind us of one key lesson, it circles back to: people who have nothing to hide, hide nothing.

Tina is smart and sassy. She's also incredibly cryptic about where she works and what she does. Although she has a degree from a good college, she has worked as a barista on and off, filling gaps of time with administrative work. Joshua has had four dates with Tina, and is growing concerned that so far she has yet to reveal where she works. As he walks Tina home, he's pleasantly surprised when she invites him up. In the elevator up to the 18th floor, it dawns on Josh that this is quite a luxurious apartment for a barista/administrative assistant. Let's eavesdrop a little...

"Are your roommates home?" asks Josh.

Tina laughs and elbows Josh, "Is that your backward way of asking if I live alone?"

"Just curious," says Josh, playfully, though Tina's right. He really is trying to figure out how a barista-turned-executive assistant can afford to live in such a luxurious building in a sought-after part of town.

"Guess you'll have to find out," says Tina, as the elevator door opens on the 18th floor, and she puts her hand on his belt buckle.

In Tina's apartment, Josh's adrenaline kicks in but he can't get over the sweeping city view of downtown Cincinnati. Torn with where to put his attention, he looks at Tina.

"Wow," says Josh.

"I know, isn't it a gorgeous view?" asks Tina, resting her head on his shoulder.

"Sure is, wow, this is surreal," echoes Josh.

"Yeah well it comes with a hefty price tag, that's for sure," says Tina.

"However can you afford it?" asks Josh, who thinks he'll have to put in even more hours at his accounting

firm if he ever wants a shot at view like this.

"My dad bought it, I just pay the monthly maintenance,"
says Tina, without skipping a beat.

"Wow," says Josh, his eyes still fixed on the city lights.

The next morning, Josh wakes before Tina and walks
into the kitchen, desperate for his morning cup of coffee.
He whips back to get another look at the city. Moments
later, as he prepares to make coffee, he's so distracted by
the view, he nearly misses the $11,000 Clover, a commercial
grade espresso machine.

"Whoa," exclaims, Josh loudly, taking a step back,
quickly lifting his hand to his mouth to mute the noise.

"Everything OK in there?" asks Tina, still half asleep.

"Yeah, sorry, everything's fine," says Josh, as he stares
in amazement. "Didn't mean to wake you."

Josh opens the cupboard in search of a cup of coffee
and finds a stack of disposable cups. He grabs one and
notices it's a typical, disposable, white paper cup. He feels
relieved but isn't sure why. No matter—it won't last long.

"Do you have to leave for work now?" calls out Tina.

"Well, soon," says Josh.

"Grab a coffee holder from the drawer on the right of
the coffee maker," says Tina. "There should be a blue
one in there," says Tina.

"Thanks!" how considerate, thinks Josh. He opens
the drawer - but the wrong one. He finds dozens of

matchboxes and several business cards. He shuts the drawer and opens another, where he finds not two but four coffee holders. "These are really nice."

"Yup," yawns Tina. "They were a gift."

"Some gift," says Josh, looking in awe at $250 Hermès croc coffee collars; a thousand bucks sitting in a drawer. "From who?"

"Pops," says Tina.

Later at work, Josh can't help but think about his luck. He'd spent the night with a beautiful woman in a jaw-dropping apartment, and enjoyed one of the best cups of coffee he'd had in ages. Still staring at the blue Hermès coffee collar sitting on his desk. *Life is good,* he thinks.

But throughout the workday, each time he looks at that ridiculously expensive coffee collar, his stomach sinks a little bit. While he'd heard of wealthy parents buying their children all sorts of luxuries, why would Tina work as an executive assistant and barista?

On one hand, he feels huge admiration for Tina, for not taking a free ride from her dad. On the other hand, something just didn't quite add up. But of all the things that bother Josh, most is his memory, or lack thereof. *Did Tina say she was a barista who filled in the gaps in work with an admin job? Who does that?* Surely, he'd misheard. *If anything, she is an executive assistant who fills in the gaps in work with a barista job, no? Yes, yes, that must be it.* Perhaps the pricey croc collars were a gift from Tina's dad to match the Clover she must've gotten as a work sample that was rejected or damaged and ended up at Tina's house. Maybe her dad also admired her work ethic and gave her the coffee collars as a show of support for his daughter's desire to earn her own way. Tina is, after all, at least paying the monthly maintenance. Still, thinks Josh, *isn't it odd that if she and her dad are so close, there wasn't a single family photo?*

He shrugs it off.

Josh isn't entirely convinced but he's a smart guy and figures he's somewhere in the vicinity of truth. Relieved, he puts the coffee collar in his briefcase and goes about his day.

Unknowingly, Josh has just committed a common mistake we've all made at some point or another. Josh just turned his head and chose to believe what was most comforting. He convinced himself of his rationale.

Josh, like most of us, doesn't want to be plagued by negative thoughts. He certainly doesn't want to believe his prize, Tina, is untrue in any way. She's beautiful and fun and she has a killer apartment and a tremendous sense of generosity, after all—didn't she see just lend him a $250 coffee collar? Most of us end up in hot water, not because we fail to see the dots, but because we fail in our desire to connect them. The small, seemingly insignificant action of tucking the coffee collar in his briefcase is also a tell-tale sign of avoidance and discomfort. The collar represented truth. Once Josh was able to nearly convince himself of what he wanted to be the truth, he put the collar away. No need to continue being uncomfortable now that he'd figured it all out, right?

Instead of relying on memory, Josh could rely on facts, to decode his mystery. Twice, Tina associated pricey items with her dad—first the apartment and next the

Hermès coffee collars. Believe it or not, finding out who gave Tina the coffee collars will be difficult but figuring out who owns the apartment is a piece of cake.

Cincinnati makes property records public. If Josh really wants to know who owns that apartment, all he has to do is look it up—for free! Cincinnati, Ohio, is in Hamilton County, which means Josh will need to search the Hamilton County Auditor database. To do this, he'll need to visit: www.hamiltoncountyauditor.org and click on "property search," type in the address to instantly discover the owner's name, sale price, and other pertinent information.

Most counties make this information readily available to the public. If you don't know which county a city is in, you'll have to take a small step back and use Black Book Online's City to County Converter at www.blackbookonline.info/bbo_citycountyconverter.aspx

Once you have the county name, go to a search engine like Google and type: Hamilton County Ohio Property Records. Another way to quickly find information on the county you need is to visit the Nationwide Environmental Title Research (NETR) Web site at www.publicrecords.netronline.com.

Now, let's say Josh were to type in Tina's address and instead of an individual listed as an owner, he received a listing for a company called John Doe LLC. Dead end? Nope. He would just have to do a free business search using the Ohio Secretary of State's Web site. He needs to technically end up here: www2.sos.state.oh.us/pls/bsqry/f?p=100:1:8415199127565405

This search will reveal the corporation details, the

agent/registrant information, incorporator information, and much more.

To get there, he can go to the Ohio Businesses Licenses Directory at www.publicrecords.onlinesearches.com/Ohio-Business-Licenses.htm

Then he'll need to scroll down under where it says "Ohio—Statewide," and click on "free search" under Corporations.

If you, like Josh, are in search of state records, you can simply replace the word Ohio in the URL with the state you need or go back to the top and select your state from the drop down menu.

If Josh had done his homework, he would've learned that Tina's apartment was not purchased by her father. The apartment was a very expensive rental. While it would not be possible to see who was paying the rent, he would've learned instantaneously that the entire building was rentals-only, which would've been the first of many lies.

Tina, it turns out, was a very well paid dominatrix with a string of wealthy admirers, also known as "slaves." The Clover coffeemaker was a gift from a client. The Hermès coffee holders, were also a gift.

While Josh and Tina didn't last past a few more dates, Josh could've been putting himself in a sticky situation. If Tina's client had run into Josh leaving her apartment, this might have caused a scene—one which Tina and her client would quickly understand and Josh might need a few seconds to discover, despite his initial gut instinct.

Remember at work how Josh thought he'd misheard Tina earlier in regard to her own work situation? He was unsure if Tina had said she was a barista-turned-executive assistant or an admin-turned-barista; neither of which actually made a whole lot of sense given her expensive living situation; rich dad and all. Seems "pops" was a sugar daddy, not an actual dad. This is another pitfall for Josh—does he want to be a boyfriend or a meal ticket?

But the dangers don't end there. Dating someone who has a sexual relationship with someone else, especially if you don't know about it, raises the stakes on many levels. Many significant others have contracted a sexual disease because of an undisclosed affair. In fact, read through some forums at www.truthaboutdeception. com for some quick sobering up.

Physically-speaking, Josh too could end up with a sexually transmitted disease. While condoms help prevent the spread of STDs, condoms are not fool-proof; in life, there are no guarantees. Moreover, there are various STDs that are passed along, even with the use of protection, such as the Human Papillomavirus (HPV). To learn about the different types of STDs and how to protect yourself, visit the Center for Disease Control and Prevention at www.cdc.gov.

And what about the lack of any family photos? That's a big clue. If Tina had never spoken of her dad, it might have gone unnoticed, but since her dad allegedly bought the apartment for which she claimed to pay the maintenance fee, it seemed unusual; it was telling. The placement of objects in our homes is a key way to get to know what's important to someone.

"Usually you don't know the exact meaning of something but the fact it's been put in that location is important. It's equally important when something is missing from the overall picture," explains Sam Gosling, professor of psychology at the University of Texas at Austin and author of *SNOOP: What Your Stuff Says About You*. "Ask about it. It's pointing you to where you know the diagnostic useful information will be. You get to know the person quickly because you are spending your time talking about those things that are important."

Gosling encourages people to really pay attention when they're in someone's space. "Look for discrepancies in the places people believe are private and public. If there is impressive high brow stuff in open public places and other private stuff in private spaces, it would suggest someone is putting up a front to you," he says.

For the most clues, turn to your date's music and book collection. "Music collections and book collections have lots of information. See how the items are organized and arranged. Are they set in place with high conscientiousness? Is it so fastidiously arranged that if you pulled a book out of place a little bit, the person would be aware of it and do something to fix it? That's leaning toward an Obsessive Compulsive Disorder," says Gosling.

Gosling and other researchers have developed instruments (scales they're called) to help people better understand one another. At www.homepage.psy.utexas.edu/homepage/faculty/gosling/scales_we.htm

you will find the:

> Ten Item Personality Test (TIPI)

> Short Test of Music Preferences (STOMP)

> Personal Living Space Cue Inventory (PLSCI)

The above site also has a link to the YouJustGetMe Facebook application. The app, created by a team of psychologists, helps you find out if people who visit your profile are forming accurate impressions of your personality. Simply answer 40 questions about yourself then see if visitors can guess your answers. The results are immediate. Afterward, visit YouJustGetMe.com to find out how similar you and your friends are and how much your visitors project their personalities onto yours.

While there are plenty of well-meaning people out there, sometimes, instruments and all, we cross paths with those people who aren't quite on the up-and-up. Susie knows this all too well.

A single mom in her early 30s living in Austin, Texas, Susie's just started dating Tim, a divorcee and commercial pilot she met through an online dating site for Christians. Tim is often unavailable on Friday nights and it's beginning to bother Susie. Still, because she's more level-headed than she used to be, Susie chooses to accept Tim into her life, hectic travel schedule and all.

One night Susie's at home, she's just put her daughter to bed when she realizes she's missed a text message from Tim. The text came in Friday at 8:55 pm. happy to see it, Susie chooses to call Tim but he doesn't pick up. Instead, Susie gets a second message that reads: *Hey babe xoxo can't talk now*.

How odd, thinks Susie. Isn't the plane supposed to be mid-flight? Curious if Tim's mid-air or not, Susie decides to check the airline online. Sure enough, the flight is listed.

She hits for a status check and finds that it's supposed to reach its destination on time. Confused, Susie sits back. *He's a pilot, he can't be texting while in-flight. In fact, the only thing he should be doing up there is piloting that plane!*

Nervous about the situation but unsure why, Susie defaults to cleaning—an old habit she resorts to in order to avoid nervous eating. About two hours later while scrubbing the countertop, Susie sees her cell phone flashing—it's another text from Tim: *flight got canceled. Wiped. Talk tomorrow.*

What? Susie goes back to her computer, looks at the flights for the day, types in the corresponding flight number and sees that the flight successfully reached its destination less than 20-minutes ago.

In the end, Tim's flight wasn't canceled. And not only was he was never on it, it turns out Tim wasn't even a pilot—he was a financial analyst for a local company. He also wasn't divorced. But how could Susie have known?

Well, there's the circumstantial evidence that triggered Susie's nervous cleaning the minute she realized Tim was allegedly texting mid-flight. There was also Tim's constant unavailability come Friday nights. But gut feeling aside, Susie could have checked to see if Tim were even a pilot. While verifying a pilot isn't as easy as calling to see if you can make an appointment with your date the doctor; it can be verified.

You can search for names of Federal Aviation Administration certificated pilots and mechanics using the Airmen Inquiry database at www.faa.gov. Just click on "search airmen certificates;" make sure to adhere to the site's terms.

Another big help for Susie would have been to conduct her own divorce verification through Texas State at www.Texas.gov.

To check vital records for another state visit the Center for Disease Control and Prevention where you'll be directed to your state's information: http://www.cdc.gov/nchs/w2w.htm

The site has a downloadable pdf version that lists costs and serves as a terrific guide.

Every state is different in what it will and won't make available. Within each state, each county differs too. This is true for marital records, licensing information, and much, much more.

If you need to check if someone's licensed and if they have any disciplinary action in their field you'll have to take a few steps back and first figure out what entity would provide their license. A quick way to do this is to use the Certifications Finder database at CareerOneStop—www.acinet.org/certifications_new/default.aspx. It provides a comprehensive starting point. From there, you can research the requirements of a job or profession in your state and continue to fine tune your search by county.

Most state Web sites will have a ton of information on different careers and vocations, the necessary requirements, and the regulating committees. There's always the Magic-8 ball approach, in other words Google. If you just can't find it type: *Texas job licensing information* in the search bar; replace Texas with your state and you'll be on your path.

Someone else who could really use getting to know her date better is Patsy. She can't believe she's scored one of Boston's most talked about surgeons, Kevin. Patsy remembers clearly when her aunt needed surgery for a deviated septum about two years ago, that Kevin was the crème of the crop. Her aunt had read of him in a national magazine that listed him at the top of his field and she was thrilled her respiratory surgery would be done by such a distinguished doctor. To this day, Aunt Sharon raves about Kevin the "breathing doctor."

Despite his accolades (all verifiable) and his first-hand recommendation, Kevin is often talking to Patsy about the high cost of living. As a freelance photographer, Patsy can sympathize with Kevin's remarks. She thinks that having one's own medical practice must indeed be expensive. Having her own office is something Patsy hasn't been able to do, but would like very much, in order show her work and meet with prospective clients.

But there's really a bigger problem forming shape and it has nothing to do with whether Patsy can afford an office. She is so excited she's nabbed this great man, a doctor, (*a surgeon* no less) and one her aunt can't say enough good things about, that she's missing all the not-so-good things Kevin is revealing about himself. Let's listen in as Kevin drives Patsy home one evening.

"A patient called the office to complain about how he's not feeling better," says Kevin.

"Is that normal?" asks Patsy, genuinely interested in learning about Kevin's work, since he's usually too tired to discuss his day.

"You too?" asks Kevin, rather sternly. "Does your aunt

complain she doesn't see improvement? How long ago did I treat her?"

"Um, I was only asking," says Patsy, taken aback.

"Is she still complaining?" asks Kevin.

"No," says Patsy, gazing at the view out the window, thinking Kevin's cranky today.

"What?" says Kevin, as if he didn't hear her.

"No, Kevin, she isn't complaining."

"How long ago did I treat her?" he asks.

"I think it was a year-and-a-half or two years ago," says Patsy, really trying to remember.

"Oh, I apologize Patsy, I'm just so annoyed with these trigger-happy patients, waiting to sue over anything and everything," explains Kevin.

"It must be so scary to be such a decorated surgeon and also have to worry about making an innocent mistake," says Patsy, leaning over to kiss Kevin's cheek.

The evening continued as usual. The days turned to weeks, which led to a near year of Kevin and Patsy seeing each other. One night, when Kevin showed up unannounced, whiskey on his breath, Patsy decided she'd had enough of his mood swings, obsessive questions about her aunt, and impromptu drinking and finally ended their relationship.

A few nights later, it was a phone call from Patsy's friend Miriam that shed some light on Kevin's strange behavior.

"Did you see that news story about a patient suing Kevin for the fake surgery? says Miriam.

"What? Kevin's being sued? What do you mean 'fake' surgery?" asks Patsy.

"Yeah, Kevin. The patient had saved up for his co-payment and was excited once and for all to be able to fix his breathing problem and he's saying that Kevin knocked him out but that he didn't actually perform the surgery," says Miriam.

"What? That's nuts," says Patsy. "I mean I believe you but that's probably one of those trigger happy patients."

"Trigger happy patients?" asks Miriam. "What's that?"

"You know, people who will sue for anything," explains Patsy, naively.

"What? Patsy! Wake up! This guy is saying he paid for a surgery that never happened. Don't you think you would know if you were operated on or not?" says Miriam, shocked she has to explain this to her usually on-the-mark friend. "And where did you even come up with the 'trigger-happy' expression?" she asks, feeling exasperated.

"Oh my God," exclaims Patsy. "Kevin told me about trigger happy and he was always so worried my aunt had complained about her surgery. My aunt! Do you think my aunt is OK?"

"I think your aunt is fine, she feels fine. And she did

take a bit to recover, remember? Maybe this is like a new thing," shrugs Miriam.

"I just can't believe this. Who does something like that?" asks Patsy.

"Well, in total fairness, he's being accused of it and people do get accused of things that they didn't do all the time," says Miriam. "But you know, where there's smoke there's fire."

"Yes," agrees Patsy, her stomach hitting the ground. "But I think it might be true. In retrospect, I think it is true."

Not long after the story against Kevin aired, other people came forward with similar claims. Patsy felt relieved to have ended their relationship.

Looking back, that conversation Patsy and Kevin had in the car held much more significance. That talk was also the first of many similar ones.

While Patsy knew for sure that Kevin was a doctor, she could have taken a few additional steps to learn more about him and his practice. After all, Massachusetts was the first state to offer a comprehensive program to give consumers access to information about the education, training, and experience of all licensed physicians.

First, Patsy could have pulled up his medical profile. All doctors are accredited and must respond to somebody, this means somewhere there is a record—you just need to find it. While the route to the paperwork varies by state, in Patsy's case, she needed to turn to the Massachusetts Executive Office of Health and Human Services (EOHHS) at www.mass.gov/massmedboard. There, by scrolling down on the left rail and clicking on "physician profiles" under "key resources" she'd be able to garner a wealth of information, such as: Kevin's business address and phone, the date his medical license was issued, hospital affiliations, academic credentials, areas of specialty, board specialties, and awards. Despite this, Patsy would need to keep in mind that this information is provided by the doctor's office. Once you pass through the first six sections, section seven starts the malpractice section. While malpractice histories tend to vary by specialty, the report on the Massachusetts physician profile compares doctors only to members of their specialty and not to all doctors. This is done to make an individual doctor's history more meaningful and is not managed by the practicing physician.

For a shortcut to the physicians' profiles page, Patsy could bookmark: www.profiles.massmedboard.org/MA-Physician-Profile-Find-Doctor.asp

The reports on this site show data for the past 10-years of a doctor's practice. It's important to keep in mind how long a doctor has been in practice when considering malpractice averages.

Some studies have shown no significant correlation between malpractice history and a doctor's competence. Still, the MA Board believes that consumers should be able to access malpractice information.

As you search for your date, or your doctor (if you're researching through a patient's lens), you'll notice an incident causing a malpractice claim may have occurred years before a payment is finally made. It can sometimes take a long time for a malpractice lawsuit to move through the legal system.

Also worth noting—some doctors work primarily with high-risk patients and their malpractice histories may be higher than average because of this. Similarly, claims settle for a number of reasons, which do not necessarily reflect negatively on the professional competence or conduct of the physician. If the doctor you're looking up has paid a settlement of a medical malpractice action or claim, it does not necessarily mean that medical malpractice has actually taken place.

As you read through your doctor's profile, you'll also find criminal convictions, pleas and admissions. This information may not be comprehensive, though courts are now legally required to provide this information to the Board. If disciplinary actions have been taken by a hospital or the Board within the past 10-years, you will see these here too.

So, by now you're probably wondering, what's not on the medical profile? Despite the vast amount of information that is available, you won't find: the number of suits filed against a physician, complication rates for hospitals or physicians, patient mortality rates, or malpractice dollar awards.

As you read through the profiles, you may find various types of licenses. Here is what they mean:

Resigned: A physician who is under investigation or named in a complaint by the Board may choose to submit a resignation and terminate the investigation. Resignations are an irreversible and final disciplinary action.

Suspension: As a result of a disciplinary action, the Board may suspend a physician for an indefinite or limited term. If the Board determines, based on affidavits and other documentary evidence, that a physician represents a serious threat to the public's health, safety or welfare, the Board may suspend the license pending a hearing on the merits.

Revoked: Revocation of a license is permanent and removes all privileges of practice. The physician must wait at least five years from the date of imposition of the action to apply for reinstatement of licensure, unless the Board permits a shorter period in its final decision.

Inactive: A physician who is inactive is exempt from the Board's requirements regarding continuing medical education credits and malpractice liability insurance coverage. An inactive physician may not prescribe medications.

Lapsed: If your physician has not renewed his or her license prior to the license expiration date it is considered lapsed. It means he or she does not currently have a valid license to practice medicine (in Massachusetts).

When you get to the criminal convictions section, remember that these criminal convictions for felonies or serious misdemeanors are for the past 10 years-only. In this section, "conviction" includes a guilty plea, a plea of "nolo contendere" (no contest) and a guilty verdict or judgment. It's important to note that the criminal issue may or may not be related to the practice of medicine.

Additional information about a physician in Massachusetts, including closed complaints, may be available by calling the Massachusetts Board of Registration in Medicine at (781) 876-8230.

To locate the medical board that pertains to your state visit The Federation of State Medical Boards: www.fsmb.org/directory_smb.html. By following the individual state links you may continue to search on your own.

In Massachusetts, if you find that there is a closed complaint or that there are disciplinary actions regarding your doctor, or any doctor, you may request information by writing to the Public Information Coordinator. There are some fees associated with this type of request. Full details on cost and explanations on how to proceed are available at www.mass.gov/massmedboard, under "Complaints & Disciplinary Actions," which is on the left rail under "key resources."

If you're in a hurry and just need answers, or don't want to search on your own, the FSMB has created DocInfo (www.docinfo.org), which provides information on physician education, disciplinary sanctions, state licensure history, and medical specialty for physicians and the majority of physician assistants. The advantage of DocInfo is that not only does it search the state where the physician is currently practicing but it also searches all that doctor's known practice locations throughout the United States. A DocInfo profile costs about $10 (see sample DocInfo report on the pages that follow).

Another thing Patsy could've done is taken a peek at what other patients are saying about Kevin. Patsy's aunt had surgery about two years ago: Patsy can now read patient reviews and also gauge if his overall likeability rating has changed amongst his clientele. Some good sites to gather opinions are: Vitals.com, HealthGrades.com, and Yelp.com. That said, keep in mind that just like you and I have friends, professionals may also have friends happy to give a rave review, whether or not they've ever stepped foot inside the medical practice they are reviewing. Use the information to gather an overall snapshot but keep in mind that things aren't always as they seem.

Also remember to look up your state's Statute of Limitations for additional clues. Every patient has a limited time in which to make a claim against a doctor. The actual time to make that claim varies from state to state but it tends to range from six months to four years. It would be good for Patsy to look up her state's Statute of Limitations at www.medicalmalpractice.com/lawsuit-and-award-limits/medical-malpractice-statutes.htm. This might reveal why Kevin obsessively asked her how long ago her aunt had her surgery.

Perhaps Kevin knows when he began pretending to perform surgery, should this be the case. Or, maybe, *just maybe,* he's watching the clock, hoping more claims don't come forward last-minute. In the case of Patsy's aunt, Kevin will have to hold his breath a little longer. In Massachusetts the statute of limitations for medical malpractice lawsuits is seven years but that limit can vary depending on the type of case or the plaintiff. That said, actions must begin within three years of the injury but there are exceptions.

Physician Profile Report Date: 06/03/2008

In response to your recent inquiry concerning the individual referenced below, the following summary of reported information is provided.

NAME/ALTERNATE NAME(S)

John William Doe, MD

J William Doe

The Federation Physician Data Center provides names previously used by reporting entities. This information is provided to consumers to assist in identification.

BOARD ACTIONS/DISCIPLINE/SANCTIONS

Reporting State Board	OKLAHOMA
Date Of Order	03/07/2003
Form Of Order	Agreed Order
Action(s)	MEDICAL LICENSE PLACED ON PROBATION
	Term: 5 Year(s)
	Additional Detail: Shall submit documentation of successful completion of the Vanderbilt boundary course.
	RESTRICTIONS PLACED ON CONTROLLED SUBSTANCE PRIVILEGES
	Additional Detail: Shall not possess any Schedule II medications at his office or directly administer any Schedule II medications.
	REQUIRED ADDITIONAL CME
	Additional Detail: CME required in pain management.
	MEDICAL PRACTICE TO BE MONITORED/SUPERVISED
	ASSESSED A MONETARY PENALTY
Basis for Action(s)	Failure to Maintain Records of Prescribed/Dispensed Substances
	Writing False or Fictitious Prescriptions
	Unprofessional Conduct

Reporting State Board	CALIFORNIA
Date Of Order	06/20/2003
Action(s)	MEDICAL LICENSE PLACED ON PROBATION
	Term: 5 Year(s)
	Additional Detail: Based on action taken by the Texas Medical Board.
	RESTRICTED FROM SUPERVISING PHYSICIAN ASSISTANTS
	Additional Detail: Will not supervise allied health professionals that require surveillance of a licensed physician.
	RESTRICTIONS PLACED ON CONTROLLED SUBSTANCE PRIVILEGES
	Additional Detail: Will not administer or possess any Schedule II drugs in office, nor prescribe, order, administer or dispense any prescription drugs to himself, his spouse, or any family members.
Basis for Action(s)	Failure to Maintain Records of Prescribed/Dispensed Substances
	Due to Action Taken by Another Board/Agency
	Improper Management of Medical Records

Reporting State Board	TEXAS
Date Of Order	11/13/2003
Effective Date	12/12/2004
Form Of Order	Stipulation And Order
	MEDICAL LICENSE PLACED ON PROBATION
	Term: 5 Year(s)
	Additional Detail: Probation is based on disciplinary action by the Texas Medical Board.
	RESTRICTED FROM SUPERVISING PHYSICIAN ASSISTANTS
	CONTROLLED SUBSTANCE PRIVILEGES RESTRICTED TO STATED SCHEDULES
	Additional Detail: Shall not dispense any controlled substances except those drugs listed in Schedules III, IV and V of the California Controlled Substances Act.
	MEDICAL PRACTICE TO BE MONITORED/SUPERVISED
	CONDITION(S) PLACED ON MEDICAL LICENSE
	Additional Detail: Shall complete a prescribing course.
Basis for Action(s)	Due to Action Taken by Another Board/Agency

Reporting State Board	OKLAHOMA
Date Of Order	07/24/2004
Action(s)	PROBATION MODIFIED - RESTRICTIONS/CONDITIONS REDUCED
Basis for Action(s)	Not Applicable

A report containing no reportable actions is just as valuable as receiving a report with disciplinary actions, because it indicates that the individual you searched against the national database has not been disciplined by a state medical board or regulatory entity. Of the physicians disciplined in 2006, 86% have held licenses in 2 to 35 different state jurisdictions.

Entities reporting to the FSMB include U.S. state medical boards and United States territories, and U.S. Department of Health and Human Services (Medicaid/Medicare). In addition, reports are received from numerous international jurisdictions including Canada, England, New Zealand and Australia.

Disciplinary actions taken by licensing and regulatory entities can vary widely in scope and nature. Actions may range from warnings or letters of concern to the revocation of the privilege to practice medicine. Actions may either be disciplinary or administrative in nature. In deciding to seek treatment from an individual who has reportable actions, the patient should closely evaluate the nature and consequence of the action and decide if the action could potentially impact the quality of care received.

LICENSE HISTORY

State Board	Date Issued	License Number
CALIFORNIA	01/01/1991	A-12345
OKLAHOMA	01/01/1990	12345
TEXAS	01/01/1992	H1234

The licensure history is provided as a resource to disclose states of past and present licensure previously reported to the Federation Physician Data Center. The License History is not to be used as licensure verification and may not be representative of current licensure status. For the most current information contact the above listed boards. Contact information can be found at www.fsmb.org

MEDICAL SCHOOL

University of California School Of Medicine
Country: USA

It takes many years of education and training to become a physician. Typically, after completing a four-year undergraduate or pre-medical program at an accredited college or university, a student may enter medical school. Once admitted to medical school, it generally takes four years to earn a Doctor of Medicine (M.D.) degree or Doctor of Osteopathic Medicine (D.O.) degree. Typically, a medical student spends the first two years in classroom and laboratory instruction (often referred to as the pre-clinical studies) and the final two years working under the supervision of experienced physicians in clinics and hospitals (known as the clinical studies) where students observe and take part in the care of actual patients. Rotations on clinical services such as internal medicine, obstetrics and gynecology, pediatrics and surgery are the foundation of the curriculum.

The Educational Commission for Foreign Medical Graduates (ECFMG), through its program of certification, assesses whether international medical graduates are ready to enter residency or fellowship programs in the United States.

ECFMG Certification ensures international medical graduates have met minimum standards of eligibility required to enter such programs. ECFMG Certification is one of the eligibility requirements for international medical graduates to take Step 3 of the three-step United States Medical Licensing Examination (USMLE). Medical licensing authorities in the United States require ECFMG Certification, among other requirements, to obtain an unrestricted license to practice medicine. Additional information regarding the USMLE can be found at www.usmle.org and additional information regarding ECFMG can be found at www.ecfmg.org.

DEGREE

Doctor of Medicine (MD)

United States medical students earn either a Doctorate of Medicine (M.D.) or Doctorate of Osteopathic Medicine (D.O.). These degree types entitle a graduate to use these initials after his/her name. The title Doctor is based upon completion of education requirements and is not an indicator of licensure status. Graduation from an accredited U.S. allopathic school program earns the student a Doctor of Medicine (M.D.) degree, and graduation from an accredited osteopathic school earns the Doctor of Osteopathic Medicine (D.O.) degree.

Currently, of the 148 medical schools in the United States, 126 teach allopathic medicine and award an M.D. degree and 22 teach osteopathic medicine and award the D.O. degree. Currently, there are not any equivalent osteopathic medical schools outside the United States. For further information on osteopathic physicians visit the American Osteopathic Association at www.osteopathic.org

In addition to medical doctors and doctors of osteopathic medicine, individuals in the United States who have graduated from an accredited physician assistant program and are trained to provide health care services under the supervision and direction of a licensed physician are awarded the degree of Physician Assistant (P.A.). Physician Assistants can provide a broad range of medical and surgical services that traditionally have been performed by physicians, such as taking medical histories, performing physical examinations, ordering and interpreting lab tests and prescribing medication.

In such countries as Australia, India and Pakistan, international medical school graduates who complete their studies in medicine and surgery earn a Bachelor of Medicine and Bachelor of Surgery degree, or in Latin, *Medicinae Baccalaureus et Baccalaureus Chirurgiae* (abbreviated MBBS, MBChB, and MBBCh.) These medical school diplomas are not offered in any United States or Canadian medical school program, and the exact name of international degree programs can vary from country to country.

Medical schools outside the United States and Canada vary in educational standards, curriculum and evaluation methods. In order for foreign medical graduates to enter U.S. residency and fellowship programs, they must first be certified by the ECFMG. In addition to satisfying the ECFMG certification requirements, international medical graduates must also have had at least four credit years in attendance at a recognized medical school.

YEAR OF GRADUATION

1985

Year of Graduation refers to the year a physician obtained his/her medical degree and graduated from medical school. The length of time since year of graduation is the personal preference of the patient and often depends on the relationship established with the treating physician.

MEDICAL SPECIALTY

* **Information provided by the American Board of Medical Specialties ®**

Following medical school, physicians may enter a residency program where they choose to specialize in a particular area of medicine, which means additional years of training. The residency program may take the form of paid on-the-job training usually conducted in a hospital setting.

During this specialty training, the residents practice medicine under the supervision of licensed physicians who are experienced in their specialty. Upon completion of their residency training, the graduate resident is eligible to take the specialty board certification exam offered by one of the 24-approved medical specialty boards of the American Board of Medical Specialties (ABMS), the American Osteopathic Association (AOA) or other non-ABMS or non-AOA certification boards. A physician may gain board certification status in more than one area of specialization.

After residency, some doctors may continue their training to specialize even further and obtain certification in a sub-specialty, which usually requires an additional two to three years of fellowship training. For example, an internal medicine graduate may choose to sub-specialize in cardiology, which means an additional three years of training. On completion of the fellowship program, the physician may take a second board certification exam in the area of cardiology.

Certification in either a specialty or sub-specialty helps the public identify physicians who have met a higher standard of educational training, passed competency examinations and have the knowledge and experience beyond the level required for licensure. Although many physicians are electing to become board certified, it is not a requirement to practice medicine. When selecting a board certified physician, it is important to review the certifying board's eligibility requirements, examination procedures, and ongoing maintenance of competency criteria. **Additional information pertaining to medical specialties of the ABMS and the AOA can be found at** www.abms.org **or** www.osteopathic.org

LOCATION HISTORY (NOT CHRONOLOGICAL)

Oklahoma City, OK   73101-5432
Austin, TX   78708-2345
Plano, TX   75094-3210
Hollywood, CA   91601-0123
Arlington, TX   76012-2600

Because the Federation Physician Data Center database is a nationally consolidated database of physician information, it is common for a single physician to have multiple locations on file. Generally, location information is self-reported by a physician to a licensing and regulatory agency and, therefore, it has not been verified. Location information is updated in our system as new or additional information becomes available. **This location history is provided for use as a guide for individuals seeking to explore additional sources of information.**

PLEASE NOTE: For more information regarding the above data, please contact the reporting state board or reporting agency. The information contained in this report was supplied by the respective state medical boards and other reporting agencies. The Federation makes no representations or warranties, either express or implied, as to the accuracy, completeness or timeliness of such information and assumes no responsibility for any errors or omissions contained therein. Additionally, the information provided in this profile may not be distributed, modified or reproduced in whole or in part without the prior written consent of the Federation of State Medical Boards.

The Federation of State Medical Boards
Attn: Physician Profiles
P.O. Box 972507
Dallas, Texas 75397-2507
www.DocInfo.org

Rock that boat

SOMETIMES WE SAY we want to know the truth but instead we wait for the answers to find us. That's how we get burned. In reality, we do this as a measure of self-preservation but it often backfires. Think about it: how many times has your world crumbled, leaving you baffled, when deep down *you had a feeling*? We often walk around cautiously yet conscientiously trying not to rock the proverbial boat, only to find ourselves neck deep in water. Next time something feels off-center, rock that boat and see what happens. If it's gonna tip, let it capsize now.

Natalia can tell you what a blessing in disguise it is to discover something one would rather not know.

Thirty-eight, divorced, and a single-mom with two small boys, Natalia has a lot on her mind. For fun, as an escape, she peruses the personal ads in the local paper, which is where she met her last boyfriend, Marc. Unfortunately, she ended that courtship when she discovered he was an avid marijuana user—a drug and a habit she doesn't want anywhere near her two growing children. Natalia, understandably, is very selective over whom she introduces to her kids.

These days, Natalia has turned her attention to Carl, whom she met waiting in line at the dry cleaner. Carl is smart, funny, and seems to be incredibly hard-working. After nearly three months together, Natalia thinks she's found someone with real potential. On a typical call with her friend Andrea, Carl comes up.

"I had the best time with Carl on that hike last weekend," says Natalia. "We climbed quickly too, it was fun and a workout."

"Sounds like things get better and better with him," says Andrea.

"Yes," says Natalia, a smile across her face.

"Have you thought of maybe letting him buy your kids those ice cream cones and building that car thing he keeps suggesting?" asks Andrea.

"Hmm, yeah I've thought about it but I don't know," says Natalia. "I mean after Marc and the pot and how clean-cut he looked, I don't know."

"I understand," says Andrea softly, "but you know, not all men will introduce your kids to drugs."

"I know, I know, it just left a lump in my throat," says Natalia. "But soon I've got to decide because he keeps asking and I'm starting to feel badly about my ambivalence," confides Natalia.

"Is there something about him that makes you

uncomfortable?" asks Andrea with genuine concern.

"Well, it bugs me that he keeps asking to meet them so much," shares Natalia.

"Oh no, stop the presses! This great guy who apparently adores you wants to meet the two most important people in your world!" says Andrea sarcastically. "The nerve!"

"Ha ha," retorts Natalia.

"He's a great guy, you've said so yourself a million times. Smart, funny, likeable. I mean, remember that time at the movie theater how you saw him talking and playing with the kids in the arcade? He's got that responsible parent look," says Andrea.

"Yeah," says Natalia, still hesitant.

"For God's sake, it's not like he's a pedophile," jokes Andrea.

"Oh my God, do you think he could be a pedophile?" asks Natalia, a veil of worry across her whole face.

"No, no! I said it's not like he's a pedophile," jumps Andrea.

"Oh, ok, well, anyway, I have to pick up Lucas early at school today. I'll call you later," say Natalia, as she hangs up the phone.

The entire 10-minute drive to school, Natalia is jittery. *A pedophile would be a disaster,* she thinks. While she'd never met a pedophile, she'd also never met someone her age who was a pot enthusiast, or as he called it, a wake and bake.

Natalia is so distracted she slams on the break and belts out a loud screech just in time to stop at the red light. *You have to focus,* she tells herself.

Later that night, her kids in bed, Natalia can't get the word pedophile out of her mind. She remembers how easily Carl went up to those kids at the arcade. *It couldn't be,* she says, trying to rein in her imagination. *Still, it couldn't hurt to know a little more about pedophilia,* she thinks, it's not like her kids will be adults anytime soon.

She begins her search on Google, following up on hits and reading many definitions of pedophiles. She discovers pedophilia is the proper term for the medical diagnosis of a psychiatric disorder in adults and is typically characterized by a main or exclusive interest in prepubescent children. Apparently, a child must be at least five years younger in the case of adolescent pedophiles for the pedophilia term to apply.

Natalia continues reading and stumbles upon www.child-safety-for-parents.com where she finds tons of information on pedophilia. The site was created by Jannie Lisonbee, a mom who wanted to protect her new baby from everything and anything possible, including pedophiles. Lisonbee says pedophiles aren't the easiest bunch to spot because many times it's the people you trust the most that you can't trust.

"Holy smokes, it's closer than you think," explains Lisonbee. There is no one picture of what a pedophile looks like, he's your plumber, your neighbor, your friend. "And it's not just men who are pedophiles," explains Lisonbee, "There are women too."

Lisonbee says there are some red flags to look for, such as:

> Is he or she more interested in your child than in you?

> If you have more than one child, is he or she giving special attention or favoring one child over another? It doesn't matter if the "favorite" child is a boy or a girl.

> Does he or she offer to babysit? (Note: there are plenty of women and men who ask to babysit who are not pedophiles)

> Does your child suddenly seem nervous when he or she is around? Beg you to stay? Lose confidence in his or her presence?

> Is your child suddenly referencing places that you haven't taken him or her to?

Lisonbee says it's important to prepare your children and instill safety principles at a young age. "Tell your kids, these are your private parts and nobody should touch them and if they do, you tell me."

On her site, Lisonbee lists several resources. Many of which Natalia found that night, like: Net Smartz at www.netsmartz.org, a site that offers safety tips and programs to teach online child safety to both parents and kids. On the Web site for the National Center for Missing & Exploited Children® (www.missingkids. com) Natalia also learns of The Cyber Tipline—a hotline people can call and report crimes against children. The tips go to the Exploited Children Division of the

NCMEC, and then get forwarded to law enforcement for investigation. The number is listed as 1-800-843-5678 or www.cybertipline.com.

The more Natalia reads, the closer she leans into her computer screen. On the MissingKids site she learns that one in seven youths online between the ages of 10-17 have received a sexual solicitation or approach over the Internet.

Determined to do more than have a chat with her kids to make sure they're safe from pedophiles, Natalia continues to click her way through the Web. She learns of keystroke recorders and GPS locators. She quickly finds her 11-year-old son's cell phone and installs an app called Find My Friends, which embeds GPS tracking software; then she does the same with her personal iPad. Being that she's the only adult in the house, she decides to download KidLogger.net as well onto the family computer. KidLogger, she's just read, is a free program that collects user activity on the computer. Now if someone were to solicit her children, Natalia would be able to backtrack and get more details.

She decides there's just one more thing to do before turning her full attention to Carl: she wants to sign up for alerts so she can know when a crime happens near her. She goes to Jail.org and enters her information and while she's at it, she decides to add the address for her yoga exercise class, her kids' school, and the supermarket where she often goes to alone in the evenings. Feeling more empowered, Natalia is ready to get down to business. Was Carl a pedophile or wasn't he?

Following more leads, Natalia visits www.familywatchdog.us and types in Carl's first and last name, along with their shared city and state. Frozen—Natalia stares at the name on her screen; it's hyperlinked and it's Carl. She can't believe it. Natalia clicks the link and a window opens revealing Carl's address. It's the same Carl.

There must be some mistake, she thinks. She goes back to the articles that led her to all these links in the first place and decides now it's time to be thorough. Carl is a great guy and she doesn't want to lose a great guy. On the other hand, if Carl is a great guy with a past history of pedophilia, she feels she can afford to lose him and fast.

Continuing her search, Natalia visits criminalcheck.com where she decides to type in her address and check sex offenders nearby. She clicks on the icons marking the homes of registered sex offenders in her area and thinks: phew, no Carl. She then quickly reprimands herself: *Of course no Carl, you dumb dumb, he doesn't live near you! Search his zip code!*

Determined to get to the truth, Natalia restarts her search on CriminalCheck and this time, types in Carl's name and state. There he is, in blue, hyperlinked and waiting to be clicked.

Natalia clicks the link and sure enough, there's Carl's photo, the same exact photo from the other site! *Oh, this is not good,* she murmurs. She reads through the information, which is much more plentiful. Here she confirms it's definitely Carl—his home address and his work address are correct. She reads that Carl was convicted for child molestation and released from prison nearly five years ago. Natalia begins to cry. *That could've been my child he did that to,* she thinks.

Shaking, Natalia next visits a site called www.Intelius.

com and pays for a full, instant, background check. The truth is, it's a lot easier to find out if someone is a registered criminal sex offender than is someone is a criminal with a record. The quickest route is to purchase a criminal record through one of the more reputable sites, like Intelius. That said, there are free resources where you can turn to, if you have a bit of wiggle room.

Take a look at your state and local corrections departments. To access a full list of U.S. departments type answers.usa.gov in your Web browser. Once there, type: *local and state corrections departments* into the search box. Now click on the first link, which should read: local and state corrections departments and choose your state. This will lead you to Web site addresses for each state's individual department of corrections and to their inmate search or offender lookup databases. Keep in mind—these are current inmates. These people are still serving time, so it's highly unlikely Natalia or you, would find a current offline suitor here.

If you think there's a chance the person you're looking for may have spent time in federal prison after 1982 you can look through online records at the Federal Bureau of Prisons at www.bop.gov. Should you suspect jail time happened before 1982, you'll need to write to the National Archives for verification. Details online at: www. bop.gov/inmate_locator/inmates_b4_1982.jsp

Despite the resources at her fingertips, Natalia is hoping, somehow, someway, this is one big, bad, mistake. And while she's aware, just like her own credit report had mistakes that there's a chance Carl's criminal record is incorrect, in the pit of her stomach she just knows. The results just solidify things. She picks up her phone and calls her friend, Andrea, she doesn't even stop to consider the time.

"Hello,"says Andrea. "Natalia? Is it you?"

"Yes," says Natalia. "He's a sex offender!"

"Oh honey, I didn't mean it when I said the pedophile thing, go to bed." says Andrea.

"No," says Natalia. "He really IS a sex offender! Five years ago he was released from prison for molesting a child!"

"What?" asks Andrea, suddenly much more awake. "How do you know that?"

Natalia knows because she took the time to pay attention to her instincts. She was uneasy about Carl meeting her kids and while she couldn't really put her finger on it—something just bugged her. It's moments like these, when our awareness is triggered, that it's worth the peace of mind to validate our thoughts. Notice how Natalia didn't label Carl a criminal after she saw him talking with children at the arcade but she remembered it. She did her homework.

The Criminal Justice system is not perfect and while there is always a chance Carl had been falsely accused and convicted, staying in a relationship of this sort is a heck of a risk for Natalia to take. In Carl's favor is the fact that he'd been out of jail for five years without another blemish on his record. Perhaps he'd changed his ways. Then again, perhaps something had happened but gone unreported... offenses against children many times go unreported as the victims, some now grown adults, are too scared, too scarred, or too unaware of what constitutes molestation and criminal offenses to come forward.

Another divorced parent in the dating scene is

Jack. At 41, Jack seems to be a great fit for 29-year old Melina, who is looking for someone more stable to settle down and build a life with. Melina, who loves children, is looking forward to the day where she has her own. As her relationship with Jack progresses, he sets a date to introduce Melina to his 9 year-old daughter, Alexandra, while she's in town for the summer. The casual meeting in the park couldn't have gone better. Melina and Alex are off to a fabulous start.

As days turn into weeks, Melina begins to learn about Alexandra, like: she loves Barbie, gymnastics, broccoli, and has a huge crush on Daniel Radcliffe from the *Harry Potter* movies.

Taking careful mental notes, Melina starts researching fun things to do with Alex (or Alex and Jack, if he's up to it). Melina couldn't be more thrilled. The little girl is sweet and spirited and Melina's future with Jack looks bright. She wants to make sure she makes the right first impression. Melina is excited to make a little time to do girl things with Alex, her head is swirling with ideas—painting pottery, matching manicures, children's museums and plays; she just can't wait.

A few nights later, alone in the car on their way home from celebrating their three-month anniversary, Melina announces she has a few surprises. Jack loves surprises.

"Ooh, let's hear 'em," says Jack.

"Well, I've got some for you and some for- hang on," says Melina. "I see I missed a call from my friend Lauren. She called several times while we were in the movie and she usually calls once and leaves a message. Do you mind if I hear the message real quick?

"Go ahead," says Jack.

Melina dials into her voicemail, pushes a few buttons, and moments later is laughing loudly. "You've got to hear this," she says, accidentally hanging up the receiver. Melina dials back into her voicemail and puts the phone on speakerphone. She has a few calls she's saved beforehand so she's bypassing each one-by-one. "I think this is it," she says, but she's wrong.

Instead the recording says: "Hi Melina, this is Aida, I'm calling about your request to bring Alex to"

Melina clicks to save the message. She's excited for Jack to hear the comical plea from Lauren begging for her tech-savvy beau to please, please, please SOS her flailing laptop, and is startled when he abruptly interrupts.

"What was that about Alex?" asks Jack, voice stern, clearly rattled. "And why did you fast-forward it like that?"

"Oh, I wanted to ask you if I could take Alex to paint pottery, it's one of my surprises for later but first I want you to hear this funny message that Lauren left for us, well for you really," explains Melina, attempting to disregard Jack's flare up.

"No, that's not it! Why did you save it? So I couldn't hear it?" snaps Jack.

"What's wrong with you? Why are you yelling?" asks Melina, completely perplexed by Jacks 0-to-100 behavior. "I can play it after, it's no big deal."

"Tell me!" he screams.

"First settle down," says Melina, raising her voice. "Tell you what?"

"You're going to kidnap my daughter, that's why you fast-forwarded that message!" screams Jack at the top of his lungs.

Melina starts laughing and begins to look around the car. "OK, what is this?" asks Melina, suddenly amused thinking this must be a joke. "Am I on candid camera?" She lifts the car visor looking for a tiny digital device or something, anything, to explain the sudden lunacy in the car. Big Top music floods her brain. Then Jack slaps her hand off the visor and hard.

"Tell me!" he yells.

"You're scaring me and don't hit me," says Melina, moving her hands away from him. Jack starts slamming the brakes, for fun, for sport. "Stop that," yells Melina for the first time "What the hell are you doing? You're going to get us killed! Stop it right now!"

"No," says Jack, stepping on the gas to outrun the car ahead, only to get cut off waiting for the light to change, like all the other cars.

Melina looks around but they're on a highway, there's no good place to pull over and get out. "Jack, please calm down and drive more slowly," she says, using her best calm and soothing voice.

"Oh, now you're going to try to tell me what to do! Who do you think you are?" demands Jack.

Melina says nothing. She stares out the window, recapping the night, trying to get her bearings. Why on earth would Jack think she was trying to kidnap Alex? *That's so deranged*, she thought. *Who is this animal at the wheel?*

> *Jack leans in closer to Melina's side of the car and this time, right by her ear, screams "You will not kidnap my child!"*

> *Melina is completely dumb-struck. She's relieved when Jack finally pulls over and she realizes that he's driven her to her home. They had initially been headed to his. As she goes to open the car door Jack tells her "I'm not coming up."*

> *"Don't worry, I didn't invite you up," says Melina, unsure what the hell just happened.*

> *"Oh," says Jack. "And we're over."*

> *"What? You're dumping me after your childish tirade?" says Melina, her eyes wide open with bewilderment.*

> *"Here's your key," says Jack.*

Melina exits the car and walks inside. In the safety of her home, she stands in the dark for a few seconds—scared, relieved, she just can't figure out what happened to make Jack so angry. And why would he think she wanted to kidnap his daughter, for God's sake?

Determined to calm herself down, she draws a bubble bath, drowns her troubles in a pint of ice cream, and gets ready for bed. Then, just as she's about to call it a night she gets a text message from Jack. It reads: *thanks for tonight.*

It's hard to tell what triggered Jack's reaction. His mood went from happy, playful, and celebratory, to deluded and seeking power and control, then back to *nothing's happened* mode with a casual text. He acted like a bully, slamming his brakes, refusing to drive normally, slapping Melina's hand, and screaming in the car and in her ear. He didn't even let Melina explain that all she wanted was to take Alex to paint some pottery—in fact, Melina would have loved for Jack to join them.

Melina thought she was left with three possibilities: Either Jack was mentally ill (perhaps bipolar?), he had anger control issues and perhaps a history of some sort of abuse, or he needed an exit strategy. *Did he have another date to get to? Was he purposely picking a fight?* While he and Melina had declared exclusivity, she began to wonder. She kept coming back to a possible mental illness.

Melina had read of bipolarity but didn't personally know anyone who was bipolar. Days later she went online to look it up and found that Jack displayed many of the symptoms.

She learned that people with bipolar disorder go through distinct mood episodes. They can be joyful one moment and manic the next. She makes a print out of a chart she finds online at the National Institute of Mental Health and turns to it repeatedly for reference: www.nimh. nih.gov/health/publications/bipolar-disorder/complete-index.shtml

Later that week, still shaken, Melina makes a bold move and calls Jack's ex-wife. When she first calls she mentions what a joy Alex is to be around and how the little girl has stolen her heart. Alex's mom says that Alex is happy to be out and about doing things with Melina. Melina feels relieved. Seeing a window, she takes it and asks Alex's mom if Jack, by chance, had ever been violent.

She learns that Jack; indeed, had been arrested for harassment but that his record was expunged since he complied with probation requirements. Jack's ex stressed to Melina that he really was a good dad though not necessarily a good husband.

Still unsure how to explain Jack's erratic behavior, Melina catches the tail end of a TV show in which a woman marries a sociopath. *Melina thinks that maybe, just maybe, Jack is a sociopath too*.

Unsure, Melina gets on the Internet to research sociopaths. First she finds a definition and learns that a sociopath is a person with a personality disorder that manifests itself in extreme antisocial behavior and attitudes, and a lack of conscience. *Sadly, this seems right*, she thinks.

She then finds a Web site called LoveFraud.com. The founder of the site, Donna Andersen, married and divorced a sociopath and shares her terrifying ordeal first-hand. She's even created a quiz called *Are You a Target*, which asks you to answer yes or no to 12 quick questions and rate how attractive a target you are to a sociopath. The questions include: "Are you willing to give people the benefit of the doubt?" "Do you consider yourself to be streetwise?" "Are you lonely?"

Hmm... Melina receives the highest possible score—she's definitely a target for a sociopath.

Unable to wrap her head around the situation, Melina finds a site called LivePerson.com that allows her to ask a therapist a question right now; it charges by the minute. Melina creates an account and sets her cell phone alarm for 9-minutes, to make sure she's done by the 10-minute mark, to keep her cost at bay. She describes the situation in detail to a therapist. He suggests that Jack's temper is a big problem and that this type of situation is only likely to worsen. He advises Melina to keep her distance.

Melina decides to do just that.

Look both ways

CREATING A DATE-A-BASE isn't scientific but it's easy and can instantly unmask a wolf in sheep's clothing, putting you in control. A quick check of an email may confirm an identity or solidify a suspicion; emailing yourself your plans, cross-checking photos, and comparing personal descriptions can save your life.

Denise, a 21-year-old college senior, wants to go out for a night on the town. She's attractive and fun, and can be quite outgoing but since she's usually studying or buried in homework, she rarely has time for a date. Now it's Friday and she realizes all her friends have made plans and for once, she's available with nothing to do.

Not big on the idea of dating sites, Denise turns to Craigslist.org to create a one-time anonymous post in hopes of finding someone to meet for a drink, maybe appetizers, if all goes well. She writes an ad requesting to meet a man in his late 20s, who's funny, easy-going, articulate, and kind; she requests a photo to trade. Denise describes herself as a soon-to-be college graduate who loves to cook, visit museums, and see improv comedy.

Denise is pleasantly surprised when she receives nearly 40 responses to her Craigslist post in less than an hour. She's also suddenly overwhelmed as there are so many responses to sort through and the night is slipping away. She decides to open only three emails and if she likes one of them, she'll exchange a few emails, have a quick phone conversation, and meet at a local bar.

Without much fuss, she picks Erik—who is incredibly charming via email and text message. Denise is instantly at ease, drops her guard, and agrees to meet Erik at a bar in town. She scribbles on a dry-erase board outside her dorm room: Went out! Finally! Don't wait up!

At the bar, she keeps checking her watch and her cell phone. It's 12-minutes past the time she agreed to meet Erik and he's nowhere to be found. *That's odd*, she thinks.

As she's waiting she notices an older gentleman at the bar who's sizing her up. Denise crosses her sweater once around as the man approaches her.

"Denise?" says the older man.

"Um, yes," she says, her eyes searching his for answers.

"Hi, I'm Erik," he says.

"Oh, you're Erik," she says, for lack of anything else.

"You seem surprised," he says.

"Um, well, for some reason you looked a little different in your photo," she says. "How are you?"

"I'm well," he says, gently grabbing her arm, "I'll buy you a drink."

Unsure what to do and not wanting to be rude, Denise follows. "I'd like a Stella, please," she says.

Denise is barely done with her first beer when Erik orders her another. She has a total of three beers before she announces that she should go.

Erik walks her to the curb and hails a cab.

"How about one more drink?" says Erik. "I know you should go but we're having such a nice time. I know this great place," he says, as he opens the cab door.

"Perhaps another time," says Denise. "I have a big paper I need to write."

In the cab, Denise wonders how she missed an age difference of more than 20-years. This man, Erik, was old enough to be her father. She reaches for her phone and looks at the photo—it could have been Erik, for sure there were many similarities, but the photo was definitely Eric at least 15-years ago.

Disappointed, she puts her phone away. As she pays the taxi driver, she sees her roommate standing outside smoking a cigarette.

"Denise? Is that you?" asks Heather.

"Hi, yep it's me," confirms Denise.

"You went out! I can't believe it," says Heather, genuinely surprised.

"Yeah," says Denise. "Didn't you see my message on the board? Oh, maybe you haven't been upstairs."

"I just came from upstairs for a cigarette; got home an hour ago," says Heather.

"Huh, I scribbled on the dry erase board before I left," explains Denise. "There's nothing there?"

"Oh, I bet one of the guys down the hall erased it," said Heather. "It's like their newest immature way to have fun," she said rolling her eyes.

Unknowingly, Denise set herself up for all sorts of trouble. The worst part? She left no trail for anyone to be able to backtrack her whereabouts. Dry-erase boards are among the least effective ways to communicate this particular type of message—especially when the board is affixed to the outside of a college dormitory door.

But let's start at the beginning. If you're going to date online (even offline, really) you need to create a Date-a-Base. A Date-a-Base is a database of your prospective dates. To create one, you set up an email address that's just for dating. This special email address shouldn't have any personal identifiers. In other words, don't use your real name, don't put your street name, apartment number, or anything directly linked to you as the email address. And whatever you do, do not create an automatic signature line for this email.

Hulahoopchamp48@yahoo.com is an example of a good email for a Date-a-Base, as long as you don't have the number 48 in your address. Perhaps you love hula hoops or were really good at it when you were younger. This is a great email because it conveys an aspect about yourself without in any way identifying you. Keep in mind, when you sign up for an email address you'll be required to enter your first and last name. This can be changed later in your settings; you may also choose to use an initial or two from your middle name and get creative with your surname. Mariacoder@hotmail.com is an example of a bad email address for a Date-a-Base, as it provides the recipient with a first and last name, with absolutely no effort. This email would be great to communicate with your friends and to use on a resume, but it's dangerous for dating. Note: If you receive an email with a first name and last name as part of the email address don't presume that's the name of the person who just emailed you; even if the name is a valid name there is not necessarily a correlation.

Once you've created an email solely for dating, send yourself an email and see what it looks like when you receive it.

Make sure:

> Your real name is not disclosed

> There isn't anything that reveals your address

> You don't have a signature line

> Your phone number(s) aren't revealed

> Your workplace is not mentioned

Main Date-a-Base rules:

> Use this email address for all dating purposes

> Before each date email yourself where you're going, with whom, and when

> Share your Date-a-Base password with two good friends in case of emergency

On every Web site that you date, register with your Date-a-Base email address. Your goal is to stream all dating-related communication into this Date-a-Base. Do not delete any emails, ever, especially if you never want to see the person again. If you feel strongly against someone create a folder and call it something fun, like "hell no," and place all emails from that person in there along with others. You can even create a designated folder for specific individuals about whom you have negative feelings or with whom you've had suspicious online interaction.

Over time you will begin to accumulate email addresses, names, descriptions, photos, and other information on your dates. If you think you've communicated with roborobert12@yahoo.com before but you can't remember, then copy and paste his email address into the search box within your email dashboard. Does he come up? No? Yet he still seems familiar? Lucky for you, you've kept all your emails. Now read through the email you've just received from roborobert12 and type in a few keywords into the search box. If someone seems familiar, you've probably communicated with them before. While some people will change the email they use to communicate with strangers, they usually stick to their wording in emails. It's likely you'll find you have this person in your Date-a-Base.

If you're dating offline, or if you make your date via phone or text, always email yourself the details to your Date-a-Base so that there's a record somewhere. It doesn't have to be an essay, a few phrases will do. Make the subject line the date. Below are some examples:

Subject: January 10

Meeting Henry 8 pm drinks Irish pub, met at dry cleaner, 5'6", brown hair, star tattoo left thumb

Subject: 8/2

Suzy Match site noon putt putt golf-Lisa's cousin's friend??

Emailing this information to your database is quiet and non-intrusive. Nobody needs to know you're on a date but if something should go terribly wrong and you don't return, your best buds will have a starting point. In missing persons cases, the first 48-hours are crucial.

Make sure you share the password to this Date-a-Base with two good friends. By creating a dedicated place with information you know it's stored safely. If you want to cc your two friends In the email, that's up to you; however, sending the emails to your friends without sending it to the Date-a-Base could prove useless if your friends accidentally delete your message throughout the day. Do not text your whereabouts, it's much easier to miss a text and there is no permanent record a text was sent; at least with email you have your outgoing message recorded as well as the incoming email—and the incoming email is bolded to reflect that it's new. Your friends are not to look in this email inbox for fun. This is a backup, a safety net. Hopefully, your friends will never need to access it; however, make sure that they can log in successfully before you start using this as your safety net.

But how could a Date-a-Base have helped Denise, you ask? Well, if something had gone wrong, her friends (let's assume Heather had been cc'd on the email to her

Date-a-Base) would have known where to look. Since Denise went on a date with someone who emailed her a photo and information, Heather would have great information to seek help. If Heather needed to, she could click on Denise's email settings and view the full header on an incoming email from Erik, which would disclose his IP address.

Every device connected to the public Internet is assigned its own unique number, which is known as an Internet Protocol address, or IP address, for short. IP addresses are made up of four parts, quadrants that are separated by periods, and look something like 108.41.22.76.

These numbers are usually assigned to Internet service providers within region-based blocks, so an IP address can often be used to identify the region or country from which a computer is connecting to the Internet; it can even be used at times to show a user's general location. In other words, a simple email from Erik to Denise could be extremely useful to authorities, if they needed to discover where Erik might live.

If you'd like to know your own IP address, visit: www.whatismyipaddress.com.

If you'd like to view someone else's, grab their IP address from their email's "full header" setting and paste it into www.ip-lookup.net. It may seem like a series of insignificant numbers but in a missing persons case it can help.

Another thing Denise could've done to cover her bases a bit better is to have asked for another photo and asked Erik his age. Just because Denise posted an ad for men in their 20s doesn't mean men of all ages won't respond. Even if Denise had made the age mandatory as opposed to a preference, it's still on her shoulders to verify as much as she can before she heads out.

Sometimes, you can catch someone in a lie by taking this simple precautionary step: When posting an ad on a public bulletin board, post a second ad as a "control post."

In Denise's case, she went to www.craigslist.org and selected her state of Georgia, then her city of Atlanta. There she scrolled down and under "personals" placed her ad under "women seeking men," and followed the prompts, selecting "dating, romance, long term relationship (ltr)" and then "I am a woman seeking a man." She then selected her area and arrived at a blank template, where she wrote her personal ad.

If Denise had created a Date-a-Base she would have gone through this process twice, each time using her Date-a-Base email address in the "reply to" field, which would automatically anonymize her information. Nobody would know Denise had posted either ad, unless she disclosed it herself. It's important to point out that once Denise receives an email from her posting, her email address will be visible when she responds, which is why it is important that Denise safeguard herself and use a special dating email address; especially since her real email address that includes her full name could disclose who she really is with a quick search on whitepages.com, zabasearch.com, searchbug.com, or countless other sites. Her IP address would only corroborate this for someone with malicious intent.

Like clockwork, Craigslist would send Denise a confirmation email that would allow her to publish, edit, and delete her ad. She'd have to click on the emailed link and agree to the site's terms and conditions.

Remember how in her first ad, Denise described herself as a soon-to-be college graduate, who loves cook, visit museums, and improv comedy? In the control post ad, Denise should play up the other aspects of her personality and write something like: hot, playful, red-head, looking for night on the town. In this control ad she should also request suitors reply with the word "fun" in their subject line so that she knows they are real people and not a spambot. This would also help Denise identify who emailed her first post and who emailed her control post—remember both posts must filter in through her Date-a-Base email for searchability and safety reasons. She only wants to correspond with men who reply to her first ad. One last thing—it's best if Denise does not post her photo on a public forum of this kind (save the headshots for log in required, dating-specific sites).

If Denise had gone the control post route, there's a chance she might have seen a different photo of Erik trickle in, which might have tipped her off about his age. A word to the wise: it's extremely common, particularly when men reply to women, that the women receive emails to both the first ad and the control ad. The main reason for this is that dating is very much a numbers game. The more people you respond to, the more likely you are to score a date. Remember how Denise received 40 responses to her ad in less than an hour? A post by a man on this type of forum may receive five responses in that same amount of time. Some of those responses may be solicitations, drag queens, and occasionally a genuine, fabulous woman looking to meet a genuinely nice man.

If Denise had wanted to verify the gender of the persons responding to her post, she could use the *Gender Genie*, which uses a simplified version of an algorithm to predict the gender of an author. By pasting an email, preferably 500 words or more, into www.bookblog.net/ gender/genie.html and selecting its genre, i.e. fiction, nonfiction, or blog, the *Gender Genie* will identify the gender of the author. The site will walk you through the rationale and even has a link to a do-it-yourself test. In a nutshell, the site uses findings developed by Moshe Koppel, Bar-Ilan University in Israel, and Shlomo Argamon, from the Illinois Institute of Technology to decode language. Apparently, women are more likely than men to use personal pronouns, i.e. words like: I, you, and she, while men seem to prefer determiners, words like the, that, and these. Men also prefer to use numbers and quantifiers, words like: more and some.

Once the text has been submitted in the search box, the *Gender Genie* will issue its female and male scores and reveal what it believes to be the gender of the author along with a complete analysis of words. While this doesn't seem too relevant in Denise's case, it could be more relevant to a man who is unsure if he is emailing with someone of the opposite sex.

What is relevant to Denise, has to do with another form of communication. Her phone! What number did Denise use while texting Erik? Firstly, she should have spoken with Erik via phone, where his voice might have indicated he was older than he had led Denise to believe. Secondly, she should have protected her digits. An easy way to do this is to set up a Google account and get Google Voice.

To get Google Voice you'll need to log into your gmail account and in your web browser type www.google. com/voice (You can create a free gmail account and use a phone number for dating purposes even if you choose to use a completely different email in your Date-a-Base—the two do not need to be dependent on each other).

You will be asked to type in your area code and whether you have a preference for a phone number (It's actually much easier to type in your area code then click to search for a number).

Once you do that, you'll be prompted for a phone number to forward calls to. Enter a number that you can use for verification. You can change this number as many times as you want later. In the meantime, you will be given a verification code. You must click for Google to call you to verify this code and punch it in to a real phone number. Google Voice has a do not disturb setting, it also enables text messaging, and is constantly adding features. For up-to-date information visit: www.google.com/googlevoice/whatsnew.html.

Now, how about all those beers Erik bought Denise? Was he hoping she'd become inebriated and go home with him? He sure made sure she had alcohol at all times.

Regardless of his plan and his plentiful supply of drinks, Denise was under no obligation to stay. Her initial reaction was that of someone who realizes they have been deceived. Erik was a *lot* older in person than in his photograph.

While no one wants to be rejected (and no one wants to be the one rejecting someone else), if you're in a situation that makes you uncomfortable, get up and get out. It's not the first time someone will get stuck with the check, and certainly not the last. A simple "I'm terribly sorry but I have to go," or "I just remembered I need to be somewhere," will suffice. Your only obligation when faced with someone who has been untruthful and put you in a precarious position is to remove yourself from it. Take your cue from a runaway bride—sometimes you just need to find the nearest exit.

No one knows more about getting the hell out than Jessica. She's swooning over Ryan, a Navy SEAL still readjusting to life after his tour in Iraq. Jess, an avid history buff, is over the moon with Ryan. Her incessant chattering is beginning to dizzy her friends.

Then one day, when Jess hears a song on the radio and strolls down memory lane, recounting how that was her song back in 2005, Ryan says "Me too! My college buddies and I loved this song."

Huh, thinks Jess. *They did?*

Unable to sleep that night, or the next, Jess begins to wonder about Ryan. *How could they both share the same song when he'd said he'd been overseas at the time?* It's not like he said he loved that song, he actually mentioned his college buddies, he was reminiscing. Jess calls a friend who also begins to wonder. Together, they invite Renee, a friend and research-enthusiast, for coffee and ask to enlist her help in digging a little deeper.

Renee's first stop is www.veriseal.org, an organization that provides free, independent, verification of Special Operations Forces personnel backgrounds to clients and law enforcement. It also responds to requests from the general public on a case-by-case basis.

VeriSEAL began in 1992 as an independent, internal unit of the Counter-Terrorism/Protection Group (CTP), its mission was to provide associates and clients worldwide with immediate confirmation of SEAL and other Special Operations Forces' credentials. That mission was expanded to a free public service in 1994 with the commissioning of the Hall of Shame—the first list of its kind to make public a roster of individuals posing as elite force operators. By using an exclusive proprietary database that compiles VeriSEAL historical case files and a complete record of all graduates of Basic Underwater Demolition/SEAL (BUD/S) training from the 1940s to current graduating BUD/S classes compiled by the Naval Special Warfare Center and Naval Special Warfare Archive, in a system called SOFCHECK. While information within SOFCHECK is not classified, it is sensitive and can only be accessed by authorized personnel.

SEALs are trained to fight on sea, air and land. They undergo among the toughest military training in the world. In fact, out of each group of SEAL recruits, nearly 70 percent fail to make it through a six-month training. A bona fide SEAL gets to wear a golden trident. It's estimated there are 2,500 SEALs on active duty, many of whom are serving in the world's most dangerous locations.

In other words, it's rare to meet a SEAL. It's also likely that Ryan is a fake.

But what if Jess has misheard? What if Ryan had said he was in the military instead of specifically saying he was a SEAL? What if he embellished his role? Well, Renee could turn her attention to the POW Network. This organization exposes people who fabricate or exaggerate their military experience. Pownetwork.org is loaded with useful information and links. The site also has links to a YouTube.com channel under the handle Buds131, which has many colorful, entertaining, and highly educational videos exposing phonies. Here is a direct link to one such video: http://www.youtube.com/watch?v=ifQOrviEgV4

Overall, military records are stored at the National

Personnel Records Center, which is based in St. Louis, Missouri.

Most veterans and their next-of-kin can obtain free copies of their Report of Separation (DD Form 214) and other military and medical records. Next-of-kin is defined as any of the following: the un-remarried widow or widower, son, daughter, father, mother, brother, or sister of the deceased veteran. Veterans or next-of-kin of deceased veterans may use the online order form at vetrecs.archives.gov (or use the SF-180).

If you are not next-of kin and you are seeking military records without the consent of the veteran or next-of-kin, the National Personnel Records Center (NPRC) can only release limited information from the Official Military Personnel File (OMPF). You may still submit a request for military records in writing. Your request must include as much of the following information as possible: the veteran's complete name, service number or social security, branch of service, dates of service, birthplace and birth date. Mail your letter (signed in cursive) to:

> National Personnel Records Center
> 1 Archives Drive
> St. Louis, MO 63138
>
> Or fax it to: 314-801-9195.

The Center will respond in writing by U.S. Mail. It can take several months for you to receive a response. The NPRC requests that you wait 90 days before you follow up. If you're in a hurry visit www.Archives.gov and click on "Veterans' service records," then choose "Request Military Service Records," then pick "Request records online with eVetRecs," and then select "Other Methods to Obtain Service Records" from the left rail. If you get lost along the process you may reach The U.S. National Archives and Records Administration at 1-866-272-6272.

If Ryan had said he'd served in the National Guard, the The U.S. National Archives and Records Administration should have information. Going back to www.Archives.gov and typing "National Guard" in the search box will lead you to a wealth of information. If you're unable to obtain what you need here, then you'll need to contact the Adjutant General's office for the state where the person claims to have served. To find the right contact for your state, visit: www.ngaus.org/content.asp?bid=142

Renee was looking for a simple yes he's a SEAL or no, he's not a SEAL type of answer. But it's not always that easy. For a much quicker, near instantaneous look, of military life, Renee could encourage her friend Jess to submit a question to a real military wife on www.marriedtothearmy.com. While these women won't be able to release any formal documentation they do know what it's like to be in the presence of bona fide military men.

It turns out Ryan was not a Navy SEAL. He did have a vast collection of G.I. Joe toys; however. Jess was lucky, that Ryan lied for an ego boost; there are many impersonators out there with evil intentions.

"A lot of times these guys get caught up in their own lie," explains Steve Waterman, ex-Navy diver and author of *Just a Sailor* (www.swaterman.com). "It feels good and they keep doing it but there are those who just want to defraud people, take their money, and run." Waterman has spent several years exposing frauds.

"More than 90% of the time people say they're a SEAL during an introduction, is false," says Waterman.

"The SEAL thing is really the hardest one to fake and the easiest one to break." He suspects that phonies will soon be everywhere, with military personnel returning home.

"Everybody is going to have fought in Afghanistan or Iraq," he says coyly. "It's just like the fake Vietnam vets," he says, explaining that although about 3-million Americans served in Vietnam, over 11-million people claimed to be veterans in the last census.

Waterman suggests people visit StolenValor.com for more information and resources. B.G. Burkett, author of the book *Stolen Valor* and co-founder of the site, is a Vietnam veteran who lost several of his fellow troopers overseas. He takes his work very seriously.

"Allowing these phonies to serve with those heroes is flat wrong," says Burkett, who's been helping the FBI and other organizations bust fraudulent military personnel for more than 25 years.

"A real vet doesn't tell you about military combat service. It's just not something they do," explains. Burkett. "Shoulder to shoulder with your brothers in that unit. Each of you had a job to look after the other. When you leave you feel guilt. You just left the game in the fourth quarter. You don't want to talk about it."

Weak economies bring out even more fraudulent so-called veterans. "It's really easy to get into the Veterans Administration," says Burkett.

Burkett says that those who are able to get 100% disability receive more than $2,500 per month, tax free. "Isn't that nice in a down economy?" he asks.

Former SEAL Capt. Larry Bailey, who co-founded StolenValor.com, and other decorated veterans have reportedly exposed more than 35,000 fake Navy SEALs.

As a precaution and a response to the growing number of people swindled by fake military men in general, The Army Criminal Investigation Unit already has issued an alert, which it particularly stresses for online dating.

Daters are repeatedly warned not to send money to anyone claiming to be in the military. Whether it's a personal emergency, leave papers, or something else that's dire, don't do it. Instead, you're encouraged to call the Federal Trade Commission at 1-877-ID-THEFT or visit www.ftc.gov.

On a side note, if you'd like to help a member of the American military who is genuinely hard at work, you may help fill a care package with things like toothpaste, toiletries, and snacks, and choose where you'd like to send it, sites like AnySoldier.com, AnyMarine.com, AnySailor.com, AnyAirman.com, and AnyCoastGuard.com are helping everyday items reach extraordinary souls.

Another type of lie is one we come across all too often. Let's listen in on Eve and Andrew at dinner. Andrew has just finished a phone call.

"Who was that on the phone?" asks Eve.

"Oh, it was Bob from work," replies Andrew.

"Geez, he sure calls at the worst times," says Eve, as she sets the last dinner fork on the table. "Come and get it."

"What?" says Andrew, typing something into his phone.

"Dinner is ready," says Eve again, kissing Andrew's cheek, and noticing he's scrambling to hide his phone's screen from her.

"Why do you always jump up on me like that?" asks Andrew, clearly rattled.

"Jump up on you?" asks Eve.

"Yeah, all I was doing was responding to Tim and you come checking on me," he says.

"Oh honey, I didn't mean to scare you," replies Eve. "Busy night, huh? Bob? Tim?"

"What? Oh... yeah," says Andrew.

"Come on, have a seat," says Eve, piling spoonfuls of food onto Andrew's plate.

Another 10-minutes go by and Andrew's phone rings again. Andrew reacts, he seems surprised and nervous.

"Damn Bob," he says. "I'll be right back."

"Sure," says Eve, pushing her peas around the plate.

Minutes later Andrew returns.

"I put it on vibrate, Bob won't bother us anymore," he announces.

"Is everything OK?" asks Eve.

"Great. I mean yeah, fine, you know, work stuff," says Andrew.

About a half hour later, Andrew hops in the shower

and leaves his cell phone on the glass dinner table. Eve is cleaning up when she hears something rattling. She realizes it's Andrew's phone and walks over to silence it when she notices he's had four missed calls from the particular number on display. She peeks down the hall and hears the water running, so she reaches for a scrap of paper and makes note of the number.

The next day at work, Eve can't stop thinking about her new boyfriend Andrew. Why was he so jumpy? And why did Bob call so many times? Didn't he feel as if he were interrupting? It seems odd to her. She tries to push it aside but can't seem to focus. Then, after a group meeting, she's walking back to her desk when she mentions the phone calls to her co-worker.

"Was it a cell phone?" asks Eve's co-worker, Alice.

"I don't know," replies Eve. "I didn't call it. Is that important?"

"You know what I don't get," interrupts Alice. "Why wasn't the number saved in his phone under Bob? Don't you save the numbers of people who call you frequently?"

"I do save the numbers, that is weird," says Eve.

"Well, first things first. Find out if it's a cell phone," instructs Alice.

"Why does that matter?" asks Alice, confused.

"Just find out," says Alice.

"How?" snaps Eve.

"Just go to PhoneValidator.com and put in his number, it'll tell you," says Alice.

Eve searches her bag for the paper with the number scribbled in it, opens it up, and types it into PhoneValidator.com. Soon enough, she confirms the phone number is a cell phone. "It's a cell," she says over her shoulder to the next cubicle to her friend.

"Great, then SpyDial it," says Alice.

"Spy what?" asks Eve.

"SpyDial," says Alice. "Go to SpyDialer.com and type in the number. Then you'll be able to listen to that person's outgoing voicemail message, if it's a cell phone that is."

"Oh my God," says Eve. "What will they think of next?" Eve follows her friend's instructions and clicks to hear the message. "Oh my," she says.

"Oh my? Oh no. What is it, Eve?" asks Alice.

Eve clicks to replay the message: 'Hi this is Roberta, leave me a message and keep it sexy.'

"I take it you didn't know Bob was female as in Roberta?" says Alice, empathetically.

"I had no idea," says Eve. "Will she know I called?"

"Oh no," says Alice. "I use this all the time to check out my online dates. Since we used the free version Bobby dearest will see a missed call on her phone. If she calls it, she'll learn she's been SpyDialed but there's no way she can tie the call back to you. Are you OK?"

"Yeah," says Eve. "Just disappointed, I was really hoping Bob would be Bob or Robert at most, you know?"

"I know," says Alice. "It sucks now but can you imagine if you found this out months later? Maybe you should give Andrew a chance to explain?"

"Maybe," says Eve, deliberating.

Later that night, Andrew calls to say he's running late. Beside herself with worry that Andrew is seeing someone else behind her back, Eve logs onto Facebook and clicks to view Andrew's friends. She types in Roberta and finds that Andrew has two friends with the name. One lives in a different state and another in their same state. Eve is able to quickly narrow her search. She clicks Roberta's name and finds her settings are rather loose. *Fitting,* she smirks under her breath.

Eve's able to peruse Roberta's wall postings, information, and photos. She then notices an album with photos describing her vacation to Peru—in one of the photos she spots Andrew. She thinks back to when Andrew went away for business and remembers how he said it was an intensive technology conference in Nevada. Eve pulls out a sheet of paper and begins to write down the lies.

By the time Andrew arrives, Eve is historical not hysterical. She's closed her Internet browser and is ready to ask him about his day and his trip.

"Wow, you're a lot later than I expected," says Eve. "Everything OK?"

"Oh yeah," says Andrew. "Poor Bob had problems with his computer so I offered to help, you know, to be nice."

Cringing in her skin, Eve's had enough. "I know that Bob is Roberta. I know that you went to Peru instead of Vegas," she says.

Andrew stares straight ahead, like a deer in headlights. "It's not what you think it is," he says. "I can explain. Nothing happened. I mean, I know it looks bad but nothing happened."

"Then why did you say it was Bob and not Roberta?" asks Eve.

"Everybody calls her Bob," says Andrew.

"OK," says Eve, "Then why did you say poor Bob had problems with HIS computer?"

"I don't know," says Andrew.

"Please leave," says Eve, as she watches Andrew close the door.

Angry and saddened, Eve starts to cry. *Nothing a little Alanis Morisette can't fix*, she thinks out loud.

Unable to find Alanis and her trusty breakup song: *You Oughtta Know*, she turns to Gloria Gaynor and ups the volume on *I Will Survive*. But it's the lyrics in the song that stop Eve front-and-center. Somewhere between changing the lock and leaving the stupid key, Eve has an epiphany. *The key!*

Eve powers up her computer and logs into her building's intranet site and sends the superintendent a message: *Please change 6H locks ASAP*, then she laughs, shakes her head, and cranks up the volume.

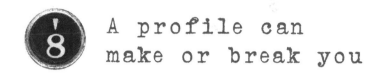

A profile can make or break you

AN ONLINE DATING profile reveals what the person wants to reveal about him or herself, not what he or she doesn't want you to know. No one says: *"Hi, I'm an ax murderer/a dead beat dad/a psychopath, let me buy you a beer."* Often, it's what's omitted that's most needed in order to make an informed decision.

Diego, a 40-year old Baltimore, Maryland, native is a sports fan; baseball, football, soccer, tennis—you name it, he's into it, but he has a sweet spot for the Orioles. Thirty-two year old Melissa couldn't know less about sports but she enjoys the energy found among sports enthusiasts, likes imported beers, and manly men. She's determined to make the most of her six-month membership to a relatively pricey dating site. Diego is one of her top "draft picks," she tells her friends. She knows her current choppy profile won't recruit her choices. She lists various chick flicks as her favorite movies, museums and art galleries among her weekend jaunts. *No, no, no,* she shakes her head. It's time to dress for the part she wants.

One Saturday, Melissa wakes up early with a plan. She stops by her local salon for a shampoo and blowout, then she goes to a high-end department store, purchases a bunch of product, and scores a complimentary makeover. About an hour later she shows up for her appointment to have a professional photographer take her photo both indoors and outdoors. She's ready—complete with change of clothes, a sports jersey, a baseball cap, even one of those oversized foam fingers she often sees on the screen during a big game.

About a week later, photos in hand, Melissa decides to give her profile a new look too. She goes on Google and tries looking up sports terminology, hoping to market herself as the perfect sports-minded potential girlfriend. A marketer by day, Melissa is convinced all she needs to do is dress the part—wear the right clothes, display the most appropriate key words, and look and breathe sports. But the more Melissa tries to sound like she knows what she's doing, the more she sounds like an amateur. *Sports fans have it so easy,* she thinks. *It's like they're born curled around a football!* She laughs at her own thought, then a little light bulb goes off over her head. No one is born knowing anything about sports. *They learn it,* she tells herself. And most people *learn about sports* when they're kids.

Melissa searches the Web using key words: learn about sports and finds a range of topics. *It's going to be a long afternoon,* laughs Melissa, getting comfortable in her seat.

A few days later, Melissa returns for a so-called study session. She spends some time re-reading the profiles of the men she'd most like to meet and realizes they all like baseball… and with baseball season coming up shortly, her choice seems serendipitous. Her profile is not quite ready for the Big Leagues so Melissa decides to turn to the pros. She finds some websites that will help her write her profile, like e-Cyrano.com, VirtualDatingAssistants.com, and also posts an ad on Craigslist.org under "gigs" to compare services and pricing. She finds someone who will not only revamp her profile but help her with emails.

Now that Melissa has the logistics underway, she chooses to further her understanding of baseball. She studies different virtual baseball games that she can play for free online, like Candyland Baseball, Gold Glove, and Bullpen Blast, and before she knows it, Melissa has switched from learning about baseball to actually enjoying baseball. *This isn't so bad,* she says to herself. She's even scoped out local batting cages and rounded up some of her non-sports minded friends for a day of guy-watching. When the women complain that they don't like baseball, Melissa steps in to paint a clearer picture: *"Then you go to watch the men, while I attempt to hit some balls. The place is crawling with men who, hello, aren't home sitting on the couch!"* Melissa's friends, convinced she'd totally lost it, decide to show a little support. Before they know it, they're battering up too.

On the way home from her day with the gals, Melissa receives an email on her smartphone from her dating assistant saying that Diego and Matthew would like to meet for drinks this Wednesday after work. Melissa is overjoyed. She decides to meet Matthew first, for practice, on Wednesday, in case she drops the proverbial ball and asks to move Diego to Thursday—to play it safe.

At the bar sipping a Belgian beer, seated beside Matthew, Melissa brings up her day at the batting cage.

Let's see what he thinks...

>*"Oh yeah?" asks Matthew. "How'd you do?"*
>
>*"Well, I hit a few of them," laughs Melissa, "But, um, they didn't go very far."*
>
>*"I like baseball," says Matthew, "but nothing beats March Madness."*
>
>*"Well to each their own," says Melissa playfully, stalling to take a sip of her drink. "Would you excuse me for a minute?"*
>
>*"Sure," says Matthew, standing up.*
>
>*"Ladies room, be right back," says Melissa, impressed that her jock-like date showed such chivalry.*

In the bathroom, behind a closed stall, Melissa fumbles looking for her phone, praying for reception. *Thank you,* she thinks as she types in *March Madness* into her smartphone's Internet browser. Crap, that's *BASKETBALL,* thinks Melissa. Now that she's discovered she actually likes baseball she isn't sure she's ready to switch from a diamond to a hoop. Not one to waste time, Melissa emails her dating assistant and asks for her profile to please be updated to reflect a love of baseball—*one sport at a time,* she thinks, wondering if baseball has any big ticket terminology that she's missed.

About an hour later, Melissa ends her date with a peck on the cheek, the same way she started it to avoid any end-of-night awkwardness. She's now set for her date with Diego tomorrow night.

After trying on five outfits, Melissa finally decides

what to wear to meet Diego. She opts to mirror his out to the ball game look and add a dash of her own sophisticated style, burgundy lipstick, and favorite go-anywhere heels. She's ready.

She arrives earlier than she intends to and chooses to sit at the bar, nursing a seltzer and lime. Melissa hardly notices the time slip by as she finds herself completely taken by the sports commentator on the large screen TV. About 15-minutes later she checks her watch and it dawns on her that her date is late. She scrolls through her emails thinking perhaps she's missed something—but there's nothing. She calls Diego's cell phone but it rings and rings until his voicemail picks up; she leaves a message.

Another 20-minutes come and go and there's still no sign of Diego. Suddenly, it hits Melissa that she's been stood up. *The nerve!* She thinks to herself. *Now what?* Just as she's pondering her next step she hears someone ask if he can buy her drink. She whips around thinking perhaps Diego showed up after all but instead is met by a total stranger, who's totally hot. Here's how things unfold:

"Oh, thank you," says Melissa. "And you are?"

"I'm Charles," he says, signaling the bartender over. "What's your pleasure?"

"Well, I'd like the Orioles to step up their game," says Melissa.

Charles laughs, "I meant, what would you like to drink?"

"Corona," says Melissa.

"Two Coronas please," says Charles to the barback.

He turns to look at Melissa.

"So, are you waiting for somebody?"

"I was waiting for my friend but I just got a text that it's a no go," says Melissa, looking away.

"Her loss," says Charles, paying the bartender for the beers. "I'm with some buddies, watching the game in a booth near the back. It's a mixed group, guys and girls but the girls don't really follow baseball too much."

"Oh, really?" asks Melissa with a slight smirk, thinking how not so long ago she was one of those girls.

"Care to join us? Maybe show the others a thing or two? We're about order some appetizers and I can never decide between the potato skins and the sliders though," he says.

"Ooh, that's a tough call," says Melissa, gathering her jacket and purse. "I vote for sliders."

So far so good. Sometimes when we prepare for an opportunity, like Melissa did, we brave for the unknown. It turns out in her "homework," Melissa learned a lot about baseball and picked up a new hobby.

Timing in life can be everything. Melissa chose to forego Diego on Wednesday so she could go on a date with Matthew and be better prepared for her date with Diego the next night. She had no way to know that Diego wouldn't show up. All that she could control were her own actions. When she realized she'd probably be sitting at the bar alone, she was forced to reassess the situation. Luckily, Charles swept in from out of nowhere and scored. Let's see how she does watching the game with the guys.

"Come on, hit the ball!" Melissa's standing up, yelling at the screen in exasperation. Charles's guy friends are chiming in, yelling alongside her.

"When did you become such an Orioles fan?" asks Charles, truly intrigued.

"About two months ago," says Melissa, her eyes fixated on the screen. "Well, he's no Cal Ripken Junior, that's for sure!" Then she freezes up.

"Are you OK?" asks Charles, noticing she's suddenly stiff.

Without thinking Melissa blurts out "How did I know that?"

Charles laughs, "Everybody knows Cal Ripken Junior is one of the few to reach 400 HR/3,000 hit plateaus. He's only the second to do it exclusively in the whole American League."

Melissa stares blankly. "Yeah but how did I know that?" she asks again, impressed and dumbfounded. She actually got a baseball fact right and it was unscripted!

"I don't understand," says Charles.

"Charles, three months ago I couldn't tell a baseball apart from a soccer ball. OK, that's an exaggeration but I had no idea about innings and dug outs or Jim Palmer," Melissa gasps. "See, I just did it again!" Charles is laughing so loudly, his friends are gathering round.Melissa, oblivious, continues. "I taught myself baseball and you know what?"

"No," says Charles, completely amused by how funny

and animated Melissa is. She's got spunk. "What?"

"I actually really like baseball," laughs Melissa.

"What happened with that 'friend' you were gonna meet?" asks Charles, playfully putting his arm around Melissa, pulling her in.

"Oh," Melissa winks, "he got traded."

A profile presents a picture and just like Melissa's profile, it can be crafted to present any type of picture you choose. Melissa meant no harm. She knew what she wanted and she was being proactive in her search. Not everyone embellishes their profile in that same spirit. In fact, men frequently lie about their height and receding hairline. Women mostly lie about their weight.

Not sports-savvy, Melissa enlisted the know-how of a sports-minded writer to revamp her existing profile and help with email correspondence. Believe it or not, it's not uncommon for people to outsource e-wooing. Not everyone presents themselves well via email and text.

In Melissa's case, she wasn't posing a threat to anybody; if only that were the case for 29-year-old Jenna. Fortunately, Jenna has a Date-a-Base to help her steer clear of disaster.

Bored and with no plans for the evening, Jenna logs on to a paid online dating site to browse profiles while she flips TV channels. Hopeful she can find a date and turn her ho-hum evening around, she posts an ad on craigslist.org along with a control post. About an hour later, her television movie coming to an end, she logs into her Date-a-Base to see what's come in and finds 53 new messages. *Probability is on my side,* she thinks.

She scans through the email addresses to see which emails only responded to her first post (not her control post) and chooses to give these emails top priority, of the 53 total emails only 9 responded to her original post.

Jenna promises herself she'll read each one and put the "good ones" into a file folder she's created within her email account called "maybe." She reads the responses. Some are riddled with grammatical mistakes while others don't even include one full sentence. Disappointed, Jenna opens one that seems more legitimate. It reads:

Hi-Saw your post on CL. My friends all have plans and it's too late to join so I wanted to get online and see if anyone else was in the same spot.

I'm SWM, 34, professional, college educated, love to sail when the weather permits. Looking to share good times with somebody. A drink at a local hangout seems top notch.

Pic attached, let me know if you want to meet up.

Patrick

Jenna looks at the photo and it seems familiar but she's not sure why. She copies Patrick's email address and puts in into the search box in her Date-a-Base but nothing comes up.

She moves Patrick into her "maybe" folder and continues to read her second-tier responses. The more emails she reads through, the more she thinks about Patrick's response. She searches for the email again and reads it once more. She's sure she's seen Patrick before.

She calls her friend to ask if she has a second to look at a photo then forwards the email. Still on the phone, Jenna asks if it rings a bell, but no.

Hmm, Jenna scratches her head, she's growing more and more certain she's seen Patrick before. She logs back on to the paid site, adjusts her search criteria, and begins browsing profiles. About two dozen images later, she finds Patrick but he seems a lot older in his profile photo than he does in the picture he emailed Jenna. She reads on, single white male, likes to read, sail, explore the outdoors when weather permits. He's divorced with one child, who doesn't live at home.

Interesting, thinks Jenna. She responds to Patrick's email expressing interest. She also tells him he looks familiar and requests another photo.

Patrick writes back and says he'd like to meet up but unfortunately he doesn't have another photo. He again makes a claim for the outdoors and this time, he asks Jenna if she'd like to ski. He says she'll have a great time.

Ski? It's July and we're in Providence, thinks Jenna. Does he mean water ski? Confused she calls her friend once more.

"Hey, so Patrick looks a lot older on the paid site than in the picture he sent me," says Jenna.

"Ugh," says Liz, "next!"

"Yeah I know, but quick question—what does he mean by if I like to ski? Does he mean water ski?" asks Jenna.

"No honey," explains Liz. "He means if you like cocaine."

"What! No way!" gasps Jenna. "Why would he ask that?"

"It's getting later in the day, it's a long weekend, you're posting an ad. Is he in your Date-a-Base?" asks Liz.

"Yeah, well he is now," says Jenna.

"Then put him in your 'hell no' file," says Liz.

"Yeah," says Jenna. "Hey what are some other terms I should know?"

"Well, there's D&D free, which is drug and disease free," says Liz.

"Yuck! Has it really come to that?" says Jenna, rather mortified by single life.

"420 is pot, gosh I don't know, I can't think of anything now," says Liz. "Next time you don't know type it into UrbanDictionary.com."

"Do you know what ice skate means?" asks Jenna.

"No, do you?" asks Liz.

"No, I just want to go ice skating this winter and was thinking ahead."

Liz laughs, "Here's an idea, put on some lip gloss and go to a real bar with real people and say hello sans computer screen," she says.

"You're so old school," kids Jenna, rolling her eyes. "OK, OK, I'll go but it makes me nervous."

"Nervous, why?" says Liz. She knows her friend isn't the shy type.

"Because I don't know anything about him at a bar. He could be anybody," says Jenna.

"You're kidding me, right?" says Liz.

"No," says Jenna. "I mean it. I don't know if he's married or if he likes to play soccer," at a bar.

"Jenna! You don't know that online either you just think you do! Wake up!"

"Hmm," says Jenna, her lips pursing in consideration. "You're right."

Patrick lied to Jenna about his age. There's no telling what else he'd lie about. He was deceitful about his status too. He said he was single, not divorced—which in essence is not a lie but since his age was untrue it put the semantics behind his single status in question.

Offline Jenna wouldn't have an online profile to look at but she would have a visual profile she could put together. Approximately 60% of what we communicate is non-verbal. Think about it, how many times have you gotten into an argument with someone and said: *It's not what you said, it's how you said it?* This means that most of what we communicate is in our facial expressions, our gestures, our paralinguistics (i.e. our tone of voice, loudness, inflection and pitch), our body language and posture, our proxemics (the amount of space between someone else and our perceived "personal space"), our gaze, our haptics (i.e. how we touch others), and our appearance (i.e. our choice of clothing, hairstyle, colors, and other factors affecting the way we look).

While Jenna may have looked at Patrick's ring finger at a bar and presumed Patrick was unmarried—she had no way to know if he were divorced or if his marriage had been annulled; nor could she tell if he were a dad. She would be able to form an opinion from first-hand experience, which is not something she could do online. It's important to remember both scenarios have pros and cons.

On the other hand, sometimes an online profile is enough to make an educated decision.

Here are some common red flags:

Bathroom Travelers: People who like to travel have travel photos. If someone says they love to travel, have a look through their photos. Do you see a phone booth in England? A victory shot atop Machu Picchu? A coral reef in Playa Del Carmen? Even if the person cannot afford to travel to exotic locations, he or she will still have photos from different parts of their hometown or city. If all you see are photos of someone using their bathroom mirror to take the self-portrait, don't be surprised if they fill up their bathtub, toss in some Epsom salt and call it Aruba.

Fake Photos: Is the main profile photo missing? Can you not view a full face? Is there a prop obstructing or masquerading the person? Why? People who have nothing to hide, hide nothing. On a dating site, everyone should have a photo and not one that they email you privately. It's nearly impossible to prove that a photo is that of a particular person and a missing or altered profile photo can be a very dangerous thing. Sites like www.verifeyed. com attempt to help.

Solicitations: If someone emails you to say they are down on their luck and could use a little cash, or if they email you to say they know 100 reasons (aka $100) why you should go out with them, do not respond. This is a solicitation. This is not legal. And any interaction can land you in a heap of trouble.

Ageists: Look at the person's age then look at their profile. Make sure the words reflect the age and the text reflects the photos. Is it a 20-something using the word gizmo? That seems out of place. A veterinarian without a single photo of an animal is quite curious. Also check the age they are seeking. If a 40+ person claims to be seeking a serious relationship with an 18+ year-old, that large age gap is questionable as well.

Ego-Monikers: "A rose by any other name would smell as sweet" is a famous quotation from William Shakespeare's play *Romeo and Juliet*, set in Verona, circa 1400. The quote means that the names of things do not matter; all that matters is what things are. Well, Shakespeare never dated circa now. In the day and age of the World Wide Web, screen names, usernames, and monikers *do* matter; they are reflective of one's personality. If you see a creative moniker that's great, if you see a million boring ones it either shows a lack of creativity or a lack of availability; however, a moniker with a person's first and last name on a dating site isn't safe and one with a phone number as the moniker itself comes across as desperate. Monikers with 'prince,' 'diva,' etc. may lift an eyebrow too. You don't want to end up on a date with someone who's too sexy for their moniker. That said, keep in mind it's not always easy to get the moniker of your choice, given the vast number of people creating online dating accounts.

Vacuums: Be wary of the profile that fills up space by pasting a vast amount of nothing, otherwise known as a vacuum. If the profile is filled with quote after quote and no real information, it's a sign. Everyone should be able to say something about themselves, at the very least a sentence or two. If that's not possible, then there's no reason to date someone who has nothing to say.

You are married?

FROM THE MOMENT you're born there are records, like it or not. There are birth certificates, report cards, medical charts, credit card statements, driver's licenses, and hundreds of other types of documentation about your status as a human being—including marriage and divorce records.

Some records are easier to access than others, particularly when it comes to somebody else. If you want to know if someone is a registered child sex offender, that's easy. If you want to check their credit record without their signed consent, that's illegal. And if you want to know if someone's married? Well, that's convoluted.

Fortunately, there are tell-tale signs and clues you can gather in the getting-to-know someone phase that can point you toward an answer, if you're willing to look for them. After all, public records sometimes contain mistakes. Sometimes, you have to look beyond a piece of paper.

Curt, is 66 years-old, a retired cop, and a widower. He thought the years of playing dating games were long gone. He believed 58-year-old Dorothy when she said she had divorced her husband several years ago. And why wouldn't he? Dorothy, or Dot, as she liked to be called was constantly busy and without escort.

New to Fort Myers, Florida, Dot instantly fit in with the outdoorsy-types. She played tennis, loved to golf, and was a regular at the country club—where she met Curt. Dot said she wanted to soak up as many sunny days as possible after living her life in the dreary Midwest. Her ex-husband, a college professor, had moved Dot and their child a few times between Kansas and Ohio for work, but Dot said she preferred living her life beachside.

It wasn't until about two months later that Dot invited Curt and a couple of her tennis friends over for dinner. The first to arrive, Curt was happy for the one-on-one time with Dot—he's had a huge crush on her since he first saw her sipping lemonade at the club.

Let's listen in on the pre-dinner conversation. Dot is in full swing and completely pre-occupied playing hostess. Curt has offered to help but was quickly ushered out of the kitchen. His first time at Dot's, he's intrigued by her vast collection of travel books in her living room. He can tell Dot must have all sorts of stories to tell.

"Is this you snorkeling?" calls out Curt.

Dot sticks her head out from the kitchen. "Oh, yes, Eddie and I went to Martinique and saw the loveliest fish," she says.

"What about this Norwegian Cruise Ship? Was that

fun? I've never been on a cruise," says Curt. "But I've always wanted to."

"It's fun till you get hammered," laughs Dot. "Well, fun for me, Eddie paid for it with quite the hangover the next day."

"Is this your daughter?" asks Curt, eyeing another photo. "She looks just like you."

"Oh yes, that Amelia, my pride and joy," says Dot.

"Is she planning a visit soon? I'd love to meet her," says Curt, trying to close the distance between he and Dot.

"Maybe, she's more of a daddy's girl," says Dot.

"Oh," says Curt, suddenly realizing that for an ex-husband, Eddie sure is in a lot of these photos. But he shrugs it off, imagining that Dot and her ex must remain friendly. Plus, not having any kids of his own, Curt feels he's not the best resource on the topic.

Just then the doorbell rings and a handful of Dot's friends arrive, Curt becomes his usual friendly, talkative, self; momentarily forgetting about Dot, her daughter, and her ex-husband Eddie.

After everyone leaves, Curt offers to help clean up and while Dot seems appreciative, she says she's got it.

"Thank you so much for coming Ed. We should have lunch and see that new Meryl Streep movie on Thursday... what do you think?" asks Dot.

"Um, I'd love to but um, I'm Curt," he says.

"I know you're Curt," says Dot.

"You sure?" jokes Curt, trying to break the ice.

"I'm sure. Why? Did I call you another name?" asks Dot.

"I thought you called me Ed," he answers.

"Must be the age," she laughs. "I'm just tired tonight," she explains.

On Wednesday night, Dot calls Curt to cancel. She says she's just exhausted and blames in on the Florida heat. She asks to reschedule for the following week on Monday. Curt agrees.

On Sunday afternoon, Dot calls to say that she's not quite up for lunch but a movie would work. Curt agrees but begins to feel suspicious. Why a movie and not lunch? Regardless, he agrees to pick up Dot at her home.

As he pulls into her driveway he can't help but think Dot looks like a Hollywood star. Her breezy demeanor and oversized sunglasses are very sexy. However, at the movie theater, Dot keeps her sunglasses on.

"Isn't it a little dark to see in here with those?" asks Curt.

"I think I have a little Pink Eye. I'll take them off when the movie starts," says Dot.

More than an hour later, Dot forgets she took off her sunglasses and when the lights come on, Curt can tell Dot's been crying for a while—a lot longer than the movie. Unsure if he should say anything, he reaches toward the floor to pick up his popcorn bin and to give Dot some time to put on her sunglasses again.

"In the mood for a quick bite?" asks Curt.

"You know, I had a really big lunch and my eye's bothering me, I'd rather call it a day," says Dot.

"Sure," says Curt. *"I'll drive you home."*

Later that night, Curt paces back and forth. Why would Dot lie about having Pink Eye? What was she so sad about? Is this why she postponed their movie date earlier? He decides tomorrow he'll pop by unannounced with some sandwiches and they can sit on her porch and enjoy a snack. *Maybe she just needs some company, she is new to town and uprooting one's life does take some adjustment,* he thinks.

The next morning, Curt heads to the local market and buys two freshly made sandwiches, some oranges, some seasonal fruit, and a small bouquet of daisies. At around noon he rings Dot's front door bell with what looks like a feast. She looks really happy to see Curt.

"What a marvelous gesture," says Dot, *"and such a surprise."*

"Oh just a quick lunch," he says, happy to see Dot's initial reaction. *"I thought we could eat on your porch, people watch a bit,"* says Curt.

"Lovely idea, I'll grab some plates," says Dot. Curt heads out to the porch. Then just as Dot's about to sit down she says "Oh! I forgot the drinks."

"I'll get them," says Curt. *"If that's OK?"*

"Yes, please," says Dot. "There's iced tea, water, and a few beers. Help yourself," says Dot.

"What would you like?" asks Curt.

"Iced tea with lots of ice," says Dot.

Curt heads back into the house, through the hallway and into the kitchen to fetch some drinks. On his way back, he walks more slowly, making sure not to trip on the steps between the kitchen and the hallway. As he steps up and looks forward, he notices one of Dot's frames is knocked over. He looks beside it and a few picture frames down there's another photo—the one that would've been the snorkeling snapshot, if Curt's remembering correctly. He doesn't say anything but makes a mental note. He's noticing Dot is rather quiet.

"Everything OK?" asks Curt.

"Oh, just lovely," says Dot. "This sandwich is delicious and this fruit, my, my."

"It looks like the Pink Eye went away," says Curt, hoping Dot will open up.

"Oh yes, must've been an allergic reaction or something," she says. "I switched shampoo, maybe I got some in my eye. I'm so clumsy sometimes," she laughs.

"Well, I'm glad you're feeling better," says Curt, noticing that Dot was running her hand back and forth slowly across her knee, the same way she did in the movie theater when she first said she had Pink Eye. She's lying, he thought. But why?

At home that night, Curt is unable to sleep. His cop instincts kick in. Something's just not adding up. Not one to skirt an issue, Curt decides in the morning he's going to talk with Dot, face-to-face, and get to the bottom of things. While he and Dot may not be an item, he'd like to be and he figures at this point he has nothing to lose but more sleep.

Just shy of noon, Curt calls Dot and says he would really like to speak with her and if she's free he'll come right over. Puzzled, Dot invites him to her home. He's there all of two-minutes before he jumps right in.

"I was just wondering if you're OK," says Curt. "I'm concerned because you haven't seemed yourself lately and I've been looking forward to spending time with you but I feel there's something I may not know."

"Why, aren't you direct?" chuckles, Dot.

"It's a cop thing I think, it stays with you long after you're off-the-clock," laughs Curt.

"Well, I appreciate your straight-forwardness and I'll tell you but I don't want you to tell the others, I'm new in town and I wanted to start over."

A big lump forms in Curt's throat. I should've run a background check he thinks. "Go ahead," says Curt, encouraging Dot to talk.

"Let's sit on the porch," says Dot, stalling a bit.

"OK," says Curt, following Dot.

"I'm not divorced, I'm separated," said Dot.

"Pardon?" says Curt.

"I'm separated. I've lived my whole life with Eddie and now he wants to divorce me and marry Rita," says Dot, her eyes tearing up. "I can't stand it."

"Oh Dot," says Curt, reaching for her hand. "I'm sorry."

"I really came down here to start over, to ease into being divorced. I tell everybody I'm divorced. I guess it's like my dress rehearsal. I keep hoping Eddie will realize he's made a mistake, that he loves me, not his new girlfriend, but last week he called to announce he's proposed."

"Oh wow," says Curt.

"My plan backfired!" says Dot, tears streaming from her cheek. "And you're really fantastic and I feel so pathetic. I'm married to a man who doesn't want me and I keep hoping he'll change his mind. He even said he wanted our marriage annulled!"

"Can you annul such a long marriage?" asks Curt. "Weren't you married more than 20-years?"

"Thirty-four! We were married 34-years and now he wants to pretend it never happened. It's bad enough that he wants it over," says Dot. "But now he wants it gone."

"Oh Dot, I'm really sorry. I can imagine how you feel. When I lost my wife it was dreadful, absolutely dreadful," confides Curt. "And this is a very big loss."

"My daughter is crushed. She left to do volunteer work overseas in hopes of wrapping her head around

the situation," says Dot, in exasperation.

"You know what?" says Curt.

"No," says Dot. "What?"

"How about we go for a trip?" says Curt.

"A trip? I don't know," says Dot. "I'm not really in the mood."

"Come on," says Curt. "Let's go somewhere and take photos, lots and lots of them, and when we come back we can frame some and start adding new memories to your collection."

"That's actually a pretty good idea," says Dot. "I could even turn a few into postcards and mail them to Amelia. I'm sure that would cheer her up too."

In Dot's case, it would've been nearly impossible for Curt to obtain information any other way. Dot had lived her whole life between Kansas and Ohio—two very difficult states when it comes to obtaining marriage and divorce records.

In Kansas, marriage records are not made public, so Curt wouldn't have been able to confirm anything there.

In Ohio, both marriage and divorce records are kept in the probate court or clerk of courts of each county. The Ohio Department of Health, Office of Vital Statistics, keeps the index of marriages that took place in Ohio from January 1, 1950, to the present day, and divorces that occurred in Ohio from January 1, 1954. These records will indicate if someone applied for a marriage license, but not whether or not the person actually got married.

If you know the name of the bride and the groom you may submit a written request to search the abstracts. If you only have one name, you're out of luck. However, you can try running a search for the name you do know on ZabaSearch.com, WhitePages.com, or any other address lookup service to see if you can find two names at one address at one time. Outdated white pages, usually stored at public libraries may hold more clues. Remember, you can pay to be unlisted moving forward but you can't turn back the clock; not on paper.

A search of this kind in Ohio costs about $3 per ten-year search per last name, and takes 3-6 weeks for an answer. Full details are available online at www.odh.ohio.gov/vitalstatistics/mrgdiv.aspx

Whenever you're searching a state that you may be unfamiliar with (and to make matters trickier you need know the county) type in the city and state in Blackbook's City to County Converter so that you can quickly move on to your next step—www.blackbookonline.info/bbo_citycountyconverter.aspx

Every state has its own rules for registering marriage and divorce information. Each state has different rules for releasing the information too.

Some states, like Florida, allow marriage and divorce records to be searched online through a company called KnowX.

Marriage records: www.knowx.com/mr/search.jsp

Divorce records: www.knowx.com/dv/search.jsp

To check what other areas are covered within KnowX

visit: www.knowx.com/dv/coverage.jsp

If you're looking for a marriage or divorce record and it's not in KnowX and you're not sure where to start, go to Google and type in: Texas marriage records (substitute Texas for the state you're seeking) and click on one of the higher up search results that's an official state website—usually it will say Department of Health in one form or another. From there the state will provide you with more leads. In the example of Texas, you'd click on this link: www.dshs.state.tx.us/vs/reqproc/mdgeneral.shtm

Aside from public records your own memory is an invaluable source of information. Remember how Curt first noticed several photos with Eddie in them? He'd also made a mental note of Dot's frequent rescheduling and the fact that she could go to a darkened movie theater but not lunch. The missing frames were a huge sign, as was the fact that Dot didn't object when Curt popped by unexpectedly for lunch—she was appreciative, she was seeking a friend. That's not to say Dot and Curt will remain friends but isn't friendship the foundation for more?

Curt felt deceived and stunned but at least Dot's reasoning wasn't malicious. More than anything, his heart went out to Dot.

Sometimes there's more to the story—and the only way to tap into those details is to ask and hope for the truth. Other times, you can gauge the situation by what you see and experience.

While walking through a farmer's market, roommates Gina and Michelle are loading up on fresh fruits, local veggies, and some baked goods they swore (again) they wouldn't buy.

"Let's walk by the dog run," says Gina. "I really want a dog."

Michelle laughs "I'm not walking it!"

"No, no, no," says Gina, shaking her head. "You've got to creative problem solve. I'm not doing research to buy a dog. I'm going to find a great guy with a dog combo," she says in jest.

"That's actually a pretty good idea," says Michelle, conceding her roommate's point. "Fine, this way," she says, leading Gina down a different path.

At the dog run the two 20-something women share a bench. "Keep your eyes open," instructs Gina.

"Eyes open- check," says Michelle. "Wait," she laughs, "Open for what exactly? What am I looking for?"

"A cute guy," says Gina, rolling her eyes.

"But how do we know if he's single or taken?" says Michelle, "I'm not that dense!"

"Well, I want a hot guy with a man dog," says Gina. "No frou-frou, yappy thing."

"Do you really want to share a bed with a Rottweiler?" asks Michelle.

"You just look," snaps Gina, "And cooperate or next time I come alone," she says, laughing so hard, her eyes are starting to tear up.

And then, as the women continue their chatter Michelle spots a man in a sweatshirt and cargo pants walking a bull dog.

> *"Hey," says Michelle.*

> *"Hey what?" asks Gina.*

> *"Hey how about him?" asks Michelle. "How do you feel about Bull Dogs?"*

> *"Cute," says Gina. "But slobbery, no? I think they drool a lot."*

> *"Well, how about that guy over there then?" says Michelle.*

> *"The one with the mutt?" asks Gina.*

> *"Yeah he's attractive and the mutt could be a rescue dog. You could score a humanitarian!" she laughs.*

> *Gina tilts her head, "Isn't that a green rhinestone collar?"*

> *"Oh, you think he has a girlfriend or something?" says Michelle.*

> *"Yeah or maybe he's gay?" says Gina.*

Just then the women hear the man calling for his pooch. "Esmeralda! Esmeralda, come here!" They look at each other and in unison say: "Esmeralda!" How fitting, they think, realizing the collar isn't just green, it's emerald green.

The women, though goofy and jovial, were onto something. The kind of dog you choose to spend your time and money on says a lot about you.

"You have to understand the different breeds and their personalities and if you do that, you can understand what the man or the woman is all about," says Bash Dibra, co-author of *Dream Dog: Guide to Choosing the Right Breed for You*. According to Dibra, while the color of a collar and a dog's wardrobe can provide insight, the type of dog itself, can tell you even more about a prospective date.

"A big guy who wants to show his sensitivity might have a little dog that's sweet and gentle," explains Dibra. "If he shows he can be gentle to that little dog, it shows his sweet side. It makes you think 'Wow, he's a nice guy.'"

Also, look at the dog and then look at its owner. Bull Dogs usually don't like to walk much: is your potential suitor on the heavier side? Basset Hounds aren't known for their jumping skills: is the owner on the calm, laid-back, end?

The American Kennel Club has a comprehensive guide to dog breeds and their personality types at www.akc.org. To decipher a mutt's personality you'll have to gauge what breeds you think it's a mix of and read more than one breed profile. Should you adopt your own dog you might want to consider some of the dog breed tests available on sites like: www.wisdompanel.com or www.canineheritage.com.

If you want to guesstimate your dog's genetic makeup, try: www.dog-dna.com. Though don't be too quick to decipher, warns Dibra. "A rare breed is a great conversation starter," he says.

If you're looking to locate the right dog for you, DogTime.com has a fun interactive quiz to help locate a good possible match. The site asks questions about your lifestyle and points you toward a likely pup: www.dogtime. com/matchup.

When looking for a dog, remember that a dog with a lot of personality has the ability to break the ice, which is great for someone with a shy personality.

"If you love dogs, it's great to get a wingdog," says Dibra, with a laugh. "If you're single you can train the dog to deliver a note to someone that says: 'want to go out for dinner?' or you can train your pup to roll over. Then you can go up to someone and say 'My dog just flips over you,' and have 'flips over' be the command for your dog to roll over," he says. Dibra, a renowned celebrity dog trainer, has step-by-step instructions on how to train your pet in *StarPet: How to Make Your Pet a Star*.

So, it turns out, Gina and Michelle were ahead of their time.

Do you know who's behind the times? Brian. He's single, 30, and shopping with a grocery list! He'd probably still be at it, if his friend Sheila, hadn't caught on.

"What are you doing?" asks Sheila, watching her friend Brian open the refrigerator and jot things down.

"What does it look like I'm doing?" says Brian, half listening.

"It looks like you're doing the worst thing a single person can do," says Sheila.

"What?" says Brian. "You're such a drama queen! I'm just making a list!"

"How many times have you been approached at the supermarket?" asks Sheila, completely disregarding Brian's insensitive comment.

"Never. So what?" asks Brian. "Women go there to shop."

"No they don't!" screams Sheila. "OK, well, yeah we do but we are also perusing the aisles for viable men."

"Well, I'm still available, list and all," says Brian, adding skim milk and butter to his list.

"Yeah, but we don't know that," says Sheila.

"Sheila, you and I already dated and it didn't quite work out. We're much better at being friends, remember?" says Brian.

"Look Mr. Sensitivity, I don't want to date you," says Sheila in a huff. "I was trying to tell you that a list makes you look taken, like you're in a relationship and you're not approachable."

Brian stops to think. "That can't be," says Brian. "How am I supposed to remember my grocery items if I don't write them down? You know I forget everything. There's no way one piece of paper is stopping the woman of my dreams from coming up to me."

"You wanna bet?" says Sheila. "And just keep the list stored in your cell phone like everybody else!"

"Everybody else knows this but me, huh?" says Brian, rolling his eyes. "Fine, Sheila, what are we betting?"

"You go to the supermarket without your stupid paper list and if a woman flirts with you then you have to take me to dinner and I get to pick the restaurant and if no one flirts with you, I'm sure it's still your fault but I'll do the same."

"You're on," says Brian, shaking Sheila's hand, thinking of all the expensive restaurants he can choose from.

The next evening after work, Brian heads to the supermarket on the way home. He grabs a cart and walks down the produce aisle, occasionally glancing at his phone for his list of items. It was then that he noticed women noticing him.

He shrugs it off as some sort of warped beginner's luck and heads toward breads and dry goods. *You see, it's not the list*, he says to himself out loud. *Damn Sheila.*

Then over his shoulder he hears someone ask: *"Who's Sheila?"* he turns around and sees a pretty brunette.

People are always looking for tell-tale signs to figure out if someone is taken or available; women especially look for signs. Sheila is right--shopping at a supermarket with a grocery list often gives the impression that someone is in a relationship. By glancing at a phone for a shopping list, you could be reading an email or doing any number of on-the-go things.

A well-dressed man, especially if consistent, can raise eyebrows. Women tend to think he's either gay or that there is another woman behind his wardrobe. Similarly, a man in a sweatshirt and jeans tends to send out a single vibe.

Call for back up

SOMETIMES WE CAN all use a little help. In case you hadn't noticed, life is full of unexpected twists and turns, and whether we enlist a professional, a service, or a trusted friend or parent, sometimes a little back up can go a long way.

Barbara knows this all too well. At 37, her parents are sick and tired of her complaints about the lack of quality Jewish men. They've set up Barbara with their friends' sons, gifted her singles trips, culinary courses, they've done everything they can think of to help Barbara meet a nice suitable man of faith. They're hoping their daughter will meet someone and start her own family like she's always wanted, but it's turned out to be harder than it looks.

Then one day, while reading an article in a weekly Chicago magazine, Barbara's mom learns about www.TheJMom.com. The site puts parents in control, allowing them to set up their adult children on dates. At first Barbara is skeptical but figures her mom has her best interest at heart. She decides to give it a go and agrees to meet a man, chosen by mom, named Jonathan.

We join Barbara and her mom as Barbara (surprised to report back that her date went well) tells her mom all about it.

"I actually liked him!" says Barbara.

"You seem surprised," says mom. "A little credit please."

"OK, mom, you did good," says Barbara. "Who's next?"

Mom laughs. "Well, I did select one backup and I spoke with his mom today. Would you like me to set it up for Thursday? And what do I tell Jonathan's mom?"

"Thursday works," says Barbara. "And tell Jonathan's mom I had a great time. I'll see him again but if he asks this time, not his mom."

Barbara's next date with Elliott goes well too. Barbara can't wait to tell her mom.

"It went so well last night with Elliott! We have so much in common," says Barbara.

"I'm glad honey," says mom. "Who do you like better?"

"I don't know," says Barbara. "What do you think?"

"Well, I can tell you which mom I like better," laughs mom.

A handful of weeks go by and courtships are progressing with both. Mom decides to do a little research to make sure both men have a squeaky clean past—and they do.

"I think I need to make a decision soon," says Barbara. "It's coming up on two months. It seems fair to choose. Don't you think?"

"It's up to you honey," says mom. "They're both pretty great."

"Which one would you be disappointed to see go away?" asks Barbara.

"Jonathan always picks such interesting date spots," says mom.

"Well, yeah, mom, but maybe his mom is picking them," says Barbara.

"Oh yeah I forgot about that part," says mom.

"The stories you tell me about Elliott make me laugh throughout the day," says mom, "and laughter's important you know."

"I wish there were a way to let someone else decide," says Barbara.

Mom laughs, "There is!" she says, "We'll let your father choose!"

"No way!" says Barbara. "I'll sleep on it."

The next day when Barbara calls her mom after work to say hi, she learns that her mom's been at it again.

"I ordered you a DNA test," says mom.

"Um, I'm pretty sure I'm your daughter," says Barbara, laughing out loud.

"No, it's for you, Jonathan and Elliott to take," says mom.

"What?"

"There's a company that tests your DNA to see how compatible you are! I found it online, it's called GenePartner.com and I ordered some kits," says mom. "Obviously don't tell both the men they're taking the test but say things are progressing and you'd like to see if you're also a good scientific match."

"I've got to hand it to you mom," says Barbara, "I taught you how to use that Internet well!"

As you can see, sometimes, having mom in your back pocket can be a real advantage. Other times, we need to find other people to call upon. If our friends aren't a good fit, or are busy, or for whatever reason unavailable, it's still possible to get a little boost. Violet is about to find this out.

Violet is 41 years-old, lives in Cambridge, Massachusetts, and is recently divorced. She's coming out of a marriage that was troubled for the better part of the last six years and she's ready to go out, have fun, and meet someone new but she's scared stiff. Married since her early twenties, Violet isn't sure where to begin or with whom. She's not sure how she feels about online dating and would much prefer to meet someone at a bar or an event. Unfortunately for Violet, all her female friends are married and unavailable for late night bar hops. Violet is starting to feel a little stuck until her friend tells her about a woman she read about in a newspaper who calls herself a wingwoman and helps people in the Boston area by introducing them at bars, networking events, and other social situations. Violet immediately scours the web and finds the news clip—she calls the woman right away. She pays $65 per hour and meets the 2-hour minimum, arranging for the wingwoman to meet her at a bar that very night.

Violet learns that having a wingwoman not only helps her meet men but makes her feel safe. Knowing there's someone else keeping watch at the bar, whom she's paid to stay there for a certain length of time, adds a sense of security.

"Do you only help women?" Violet asks her wingwoman, Rocio.

"Oh no," says Rocio. "We help men too. They can be just as shy."

"Huh," says Violet, "My husband wasn't shy," she says, sarcastically, referring to her ex's infidelity.

"I'm sorry," says Rocio. "But yes, there are a lot of shy men out there and many of them are such great dates!"

"Why do you think they're so shy?" asks Violet.

"Well, if they've approached someone who wasn't interested sometimes they internalize it and it's hard for them to move on," explains Rocio. "Women are much better at 'getting over it' and will often get a

new haircut, buy a new sexy outfit. They tend to be more proactive, I find."

Violet is so entrenched in the conversation she completely misses the men that are eyeing her, then she notices Rocio spring into action.

"Hi," she says, tapping one of the men who just gazed at Violet on the shoulder. The man turns around. "My friend here was hoping you could help us clear something up," says Rocio. Violet suddenly feels a huge lump in her throat. "She was wondering how you pronounce the name of this pub. It's an Irish place, as you can see, and she thought you were cute enough to be Irish."

Violet looks at Rocio, eyes big, like she wants to die of embarrassment. Then she hears the man laugh, say he's flattered, and pronounce the name of the pub as best he can. He moves in closer to Violet. Rocio nudges her so the man can't see.

"I'm Violet," she says.

And just like that, Violet is off to a running start. Sometimes we all need someone else to give us a little kick.

Susan Baxter, founder of Hireabostonwingwoman. com says "Our job is to give it 100 percent. We also try to boost confidence too if someone's feeling insecure and is not super outgoing, it's our job to put that special person in the spotlight and be a commercial for that woman or man in a way."

But what if you're not ready for a kick, you ask? What

if you're swimming in indecision? Well then, how about a game of cards. Yes, cards?

Dr. Elsbeth Martindale, a licensed psychologist, developed a deck of cards with questions to ask yourself while dating to see if you are on the right track toward finding love. Her Things to Know Before You Say "Go" card deck consists of 76 cards (and an accompanying book). Each card contains an important question to ask during the beginning, middle, and commitment phases of a relationship.

There is a main question on the front of each card and extended questions on the back. The book explains why each question should not be neglected before giving your heart away. If you want to know if the person you are dating is the "right" person for you, you can buy the deck, sort your responses, and see how your relationship stacks up to your values and desires. Dr. Martindale sells the cards on her site ($29.95) at www.CourageToBloom.com. She's also developed the deck into an iPhone app called The Questions, so you can take all the wisdom from the deck to-go. The app lets you personalize the questions by typing in the name and gender of the person you're personally investigating/evaluating for a relationship and is available for $3.99 at the iTunes store.

Apps can help you find clarity and even safety. Seventeen-year-old Katie, fortunately, is prepared. She's on a usual date with Trevor, a boy her age, from a neighboring high school. A teenager at heart, she lied and told her parents she was meeting her friend Sasha for a movie at the mall.

Later, in the backseat of Trevor's car, Katie realizes she's in over her head. She wanted alone-time with Trevor and she did want things to progress intimately, but now she's not so sure. She doesn't like that she's in the back seat of his second-hand car. She doesn't like that she lied to her parents and she really doesn't like how pushy Trevor has become.

> *"I think we should slow it down," says Katie, as Trevor traces her bra strap outside her blouse.*
>
> *"Why?" asks Trevor, not stopping.*
>
> *"I don't know," says Katie. "I just want to slow down."*
>
> *"You said you wanted this," says Trevor, unbuttoning her blouse.*
>
> *"Well, now I want to stop," says Katie, sitting up.*
>
> *"Come on, Katie!" yells Trevor. "You're just nervous."*
>
> *"Yeah I am nervous," says Katie, "But I also want to stop. Take me home."*
>
> *"No," says Trevor, kissing the nape of Katie's neck. She starts to push Trevor but his body weight is getting heavier and more restrictive. Katie starts to panic.*

Then out of the corner of her eye she sees an SOS locator poking out of her purse pocket. Katie's parents had bought her a Teen SOS locator to help in case of an emergency, after a young child had been abducted at a bus stop several towns over. Katie had thought them paranoid but just about now she thought that gadget might be what she needed to stop Trevor without calling the cops and causing a huge scene.

> *"Trevor, stop right now! I mean it!" says Katie, starting*

to cry, her hands trembling.

"Calm down Katie, you're going to like it," says Trevor, putting his hand over her mouth. Katie breathes and waits a moment for Trevor to resume, then she uses her free arm to grab the button and holds it down for a few seconds. Trevor doesn't know it yet but she's sent a text message with her GPS coordinates to both her mom and dad.

"That's a good girl, Katie. I'm going to remove my hand. Just cooperate and everything will be fine."

"My parents will be here any second," says Katie. "I pressed my SOS."

"Shit!" says Trevor, scrambling to the front seat. "Get out!" he yells at Katie, opening the door, and pushing her out the backside.

Alone and scared, in some random parking lot at night, Katie calls her mom, who is already on her way with Katie's dad to her location. She tells her parents what happened—the truth this time. She figures she's in a lot of trouble at home but it's a lot less trouble than she almost ended up in.

Locateloveones.com (note: it's love ones in the URL not loved ones) sells and rents a Teen SOS locator that allows a teen, or anyone using it, to press a button and have two-way communication. The locator will also allow someone whose number is registered with the locator to listen in on what's happening (without ringing like a phone would) so it's important that you check with your state's privacy laws regarding use. The system is GPS enabled, which allowed Katie's parents to know exactly where she was located.

the location. You'll receive a follow up email asking for details. Once it's complete, the alleged violator's photo and your story are posted on the company's Web site at www.ihollaback.org for all to see (free on iTunes).

Despite all the apps and resources and Web sites, nothing beats good old-fashioned common sense.

So, the next time you have a hunch, explore it. You don't need to perform a thousand-step check on each and every date, but dig a little. And if something seems off, dig a lot.

Keep your sense of humor, have a laugh at the RejectionLine.com, take a peek at your astrological compatibility on Moonit.com, or see if anyone's new on Cheaterville.com, but remember that karma means business. What goes around, comes around—so take the high road. Learn when to back away from your keyboard and remember to keep your chin up; not only when times are tough but *especially* when times are at their worst.

"Whatever bad experience you had in a relationship, don't allow it to define the rest of your future relationships," says Dr. Mildred Borras, a psychologist based in New York City. "Use that knowledge to make better choices and to build your confidence. Never give someone who betrayed you so much power in your life."

Dr. Borras encourages her patients to regain control of their situations. "Be adult-like, be mature, respond to negative experiences as growing challenges and not as a victim," she says.

And, well, just like that, you too can turn a page, and then a couple more. Before you know it you've hit the end of a chapter and the start of the something new. Who knows, maybe you write a book? Or maybe, *just maybe,* you'll find yourself suddenly in a hurry trying to bend a ruler (which never works), looking for your ring size, as you stumble on www.findmyringsize.com. *How do they come up with stuff?* Who knows? But you know what? If the ring *really* fits, wear it.

Despite the erroneous consensus, I am not anti-marriage. I am pro-damn sure.

Don't go
Stay in the *loupe*

Find InvestiDate on Facebook

Follow @InvestiDate on Twitter

Sign up for a free electronic newsletter with tips
www.investidateyourdate.com/FREE-e-newsletter.html

Read the latest 007-style clues
www.investidateyourdate.com/blog.html

Catch a quick how-to video and get to work
www.youtube.com/user/Investidate

Take a webinar from home *in your pajamas*
www.investidateyourdate.com/Classes.html

Join us for an in-person workshop
(regular clothing required)
www.investidateyourdate.com/Classes.html

In NYC? Become a Secret Agent!
www.meetup.com/Secret-Agents

Have a story or thought to share? I'd love to hear from
you! Email investidate@gmail.com

Made in the USA
Lexington, KY
13 July 2012